PIANO • VOCAL • GUITAR

BEAUTIFUL BALLADS

ISBN 978-1-5400-0396-6

7777 W. BLUEMOUND RD. P.O. BOX 13819 MILWAUKEE, WI 53213

Visit Hal Leonard Online at
www.halleonard.com

4   ALL OF ME • John Legend

10   BLESS THE BROKEN ROAD • Rascal Flatts

24   BRIDGE OVER TROUBLED WATER • Simon & Garfunkel

17   CANDLE IN THE WIND • Elton John

30   DON'T KNOW MUCH • Aaron Neville & Linda Ronstadt

36   FIELDS OF GOLD • Sting

44   FIRE AND RAIN • James Taylor

41   HALLELUJAH • Leonard Cohen, Jeff Buckley

48   HAVE I TOLD YOU LATELY • Rod Stewart

53   (EVERYTHING I DO) I DO IT FOR YOU • Bryan Adams

58   IMAGINE • John Lennon

62   JUST THE WAY YOU ARE • Billy Joel

71   KILLING ME SOFTLY WITH HIS SONG • Roberta Flack, Fugees

74   THE LONG AND WINDING ROAD • The Beatles

78   MORE THAN WORDS • Extreme

84   MY HEART WILL GO ON • Celine Dion
(LOVE THEME FROM 'TITANIC')

90   SAY SOMETHING • A Great Big World & Christina Aguilera

102   SOMEONE LIKE YOU • Adele

110   STAY WITH ME • Sam Smith

97   TEARS IN HEAVEN • Eric Clapton

140   THINKING OUT LOUD • Ed Sheeran

114   TIME IN A BOTTLE • Jim Croce

118   TRUE COLORS • Cyndi Lauper, Phil Collins

124   UP WHERE WE BELONG • Joe Cocker & Jennifer Warnes

128   YOU RAISE ME UP • Josh Groban

134   YOU'VE GOT A FRIEND • Carole King, James Taylor

ALL OF ME

Words and Music by JOHN STEPHENS
and TOBY GAD

Moderately, with feeling

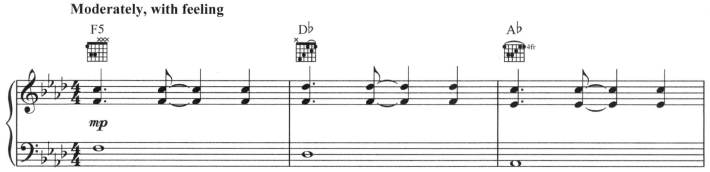

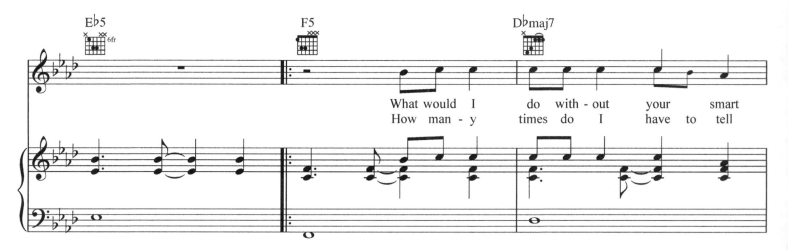

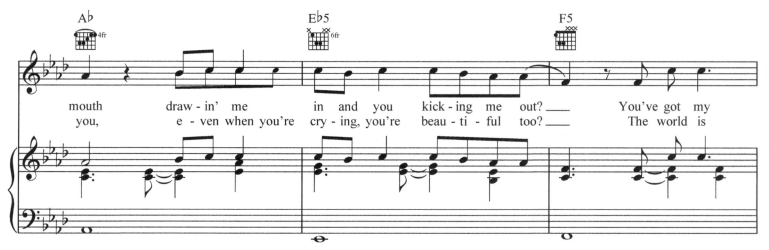

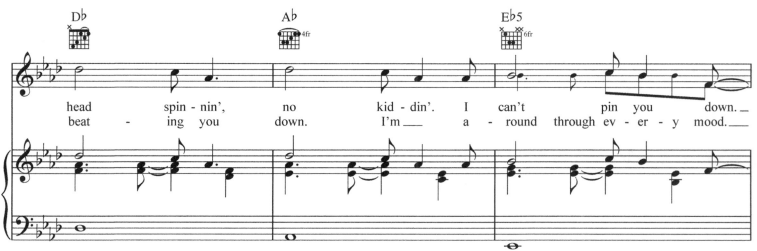

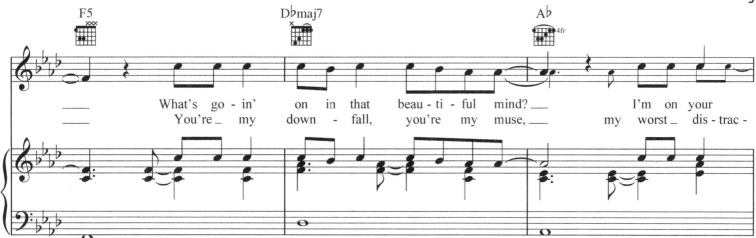

What's go-in' on in that beau-ti-ful mind? ___ I'm on your
You're __ my down - fall, you're my muse, ___ my worst __ dis-trac-

mag - i - cal mys - ter - y ride. ___ And I'm so diz - zy; don't
- tion, my rhy - thm and blues. ___ I can't stop sing - in', ___ it's

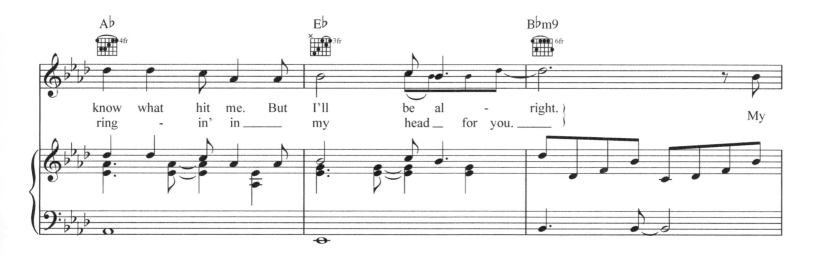

know what hit me. But I'll be al - right.
ring - in' in ___ my head __ for you. ___ My

head's un - der wa - ter, ___ but I'm ___ breath - ing fine. __

You're _____ cra - zy and I'm _____ out _____ of my mind. _____

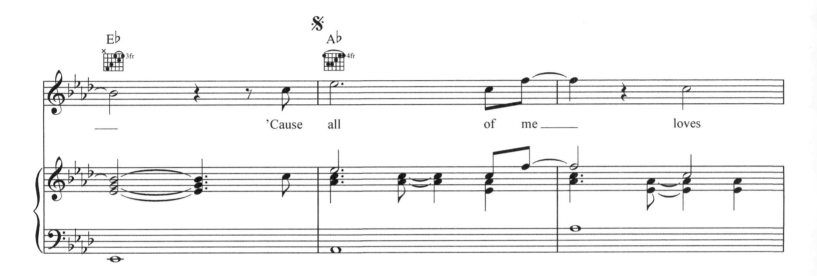

'Cause all _____ of me _____ loves

all _____ of you. _____ Love your curves and all your edg -

es, all your per - fect im - per - fec - tions. Give your

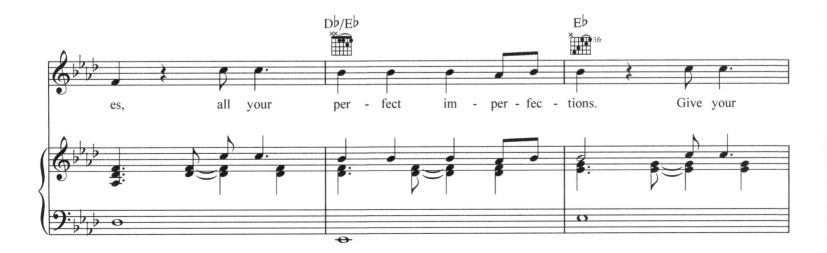

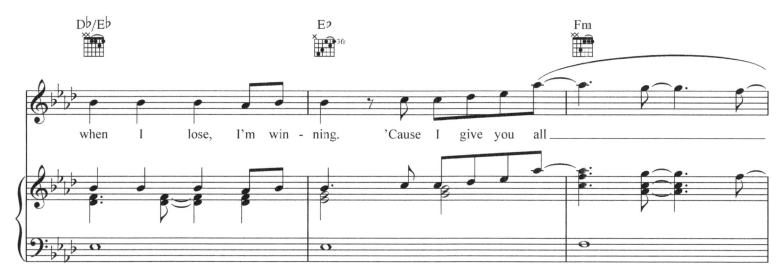

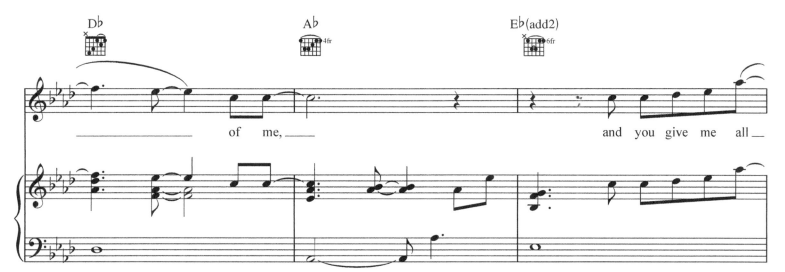

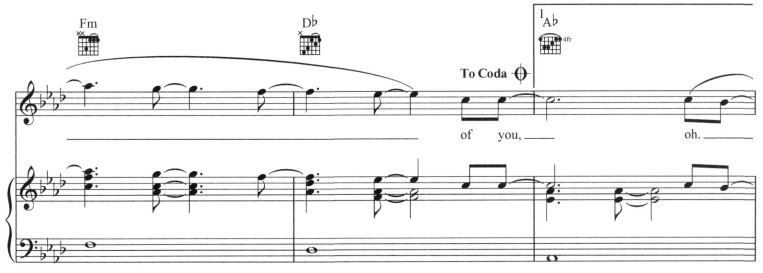

of you, _____ oh. _____

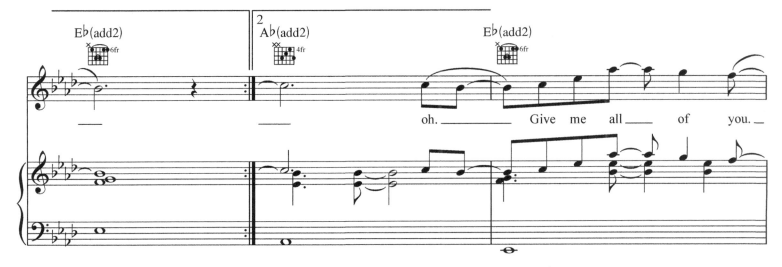

_____ _____ oh. _____ Give me all ___ of you. ___

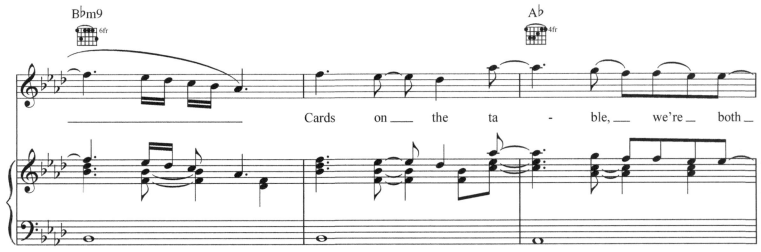

_____ Cards on ___ the ta - ble, ___ we're ___ both ___

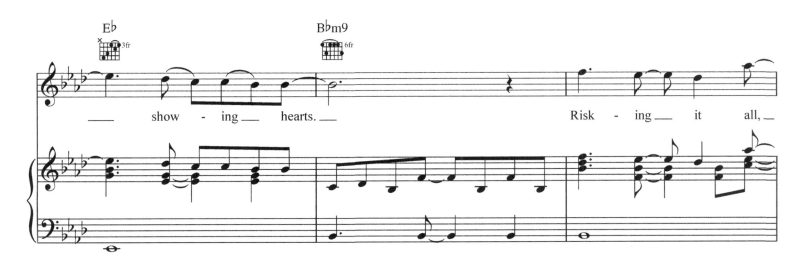

___ show - ing ___ hearts. ___ Risk - ing ___ it all, ___

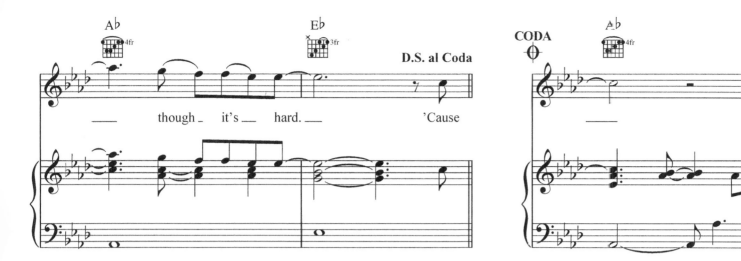

though_ it's_ hard.__ 'Cause

D.S. al Coda

CODA

I give you all _____ of me,_

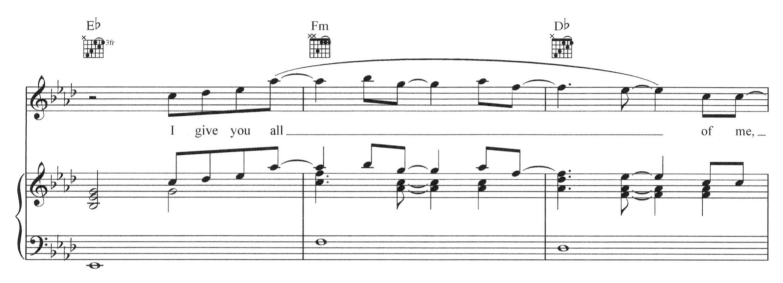

___ and you give me all _____

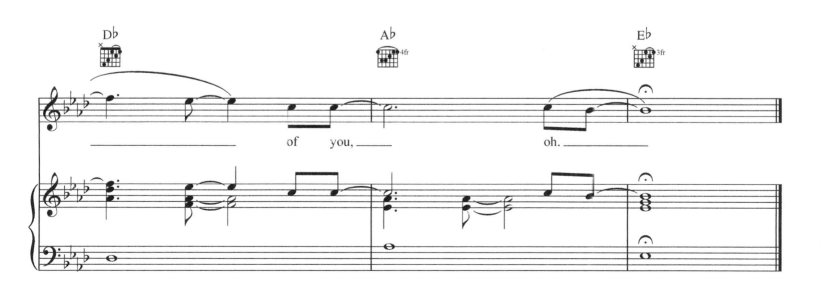

_____ of you,_____ oh._____

BLESS THE BROKEN ROAD

Words and Music by MARCUS HUMMON,
BOBBY BOYD and JEFF HANNA

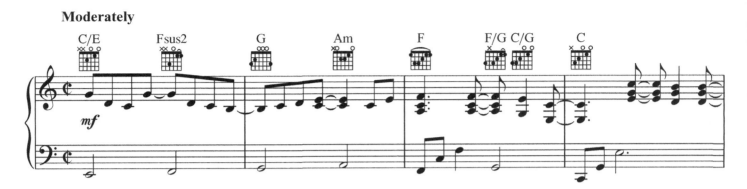

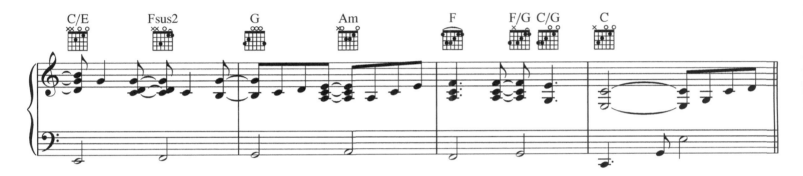

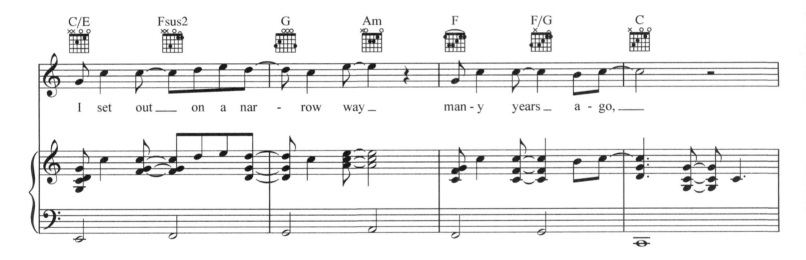

I set out ___ on a nar-row way ___ man-y years ___ a - go, ___

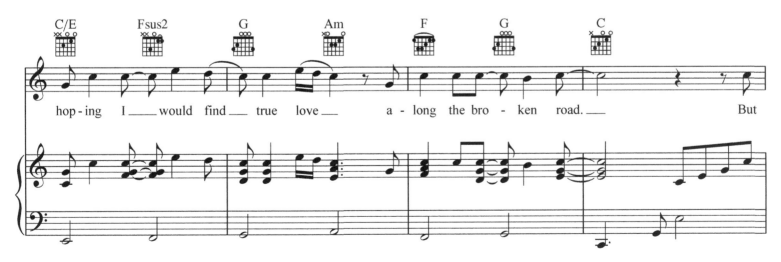

hop - ing I ___ would find ___ true love ___ a - long the bro - ken road. ___ But

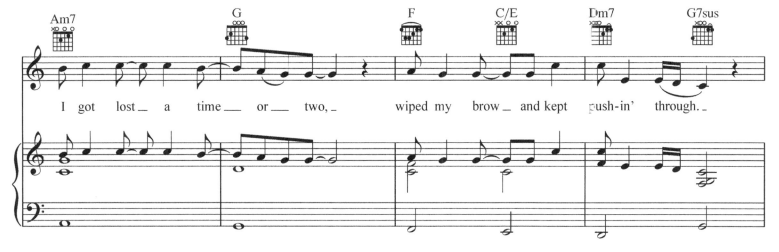

I got lost __ a time __ or __ two, __ wiped my brow __ and kept push-in' through. __

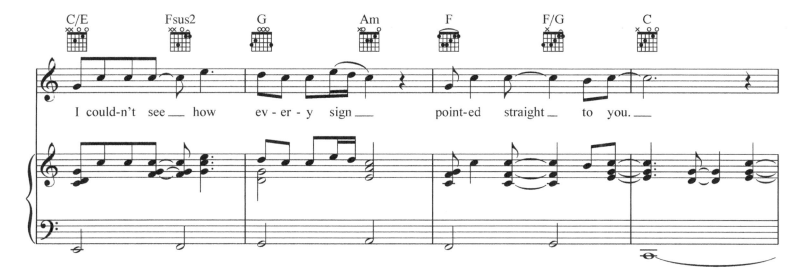

I could-n't see __ how ev - er - y sign __ point-ed straight __ to you. __

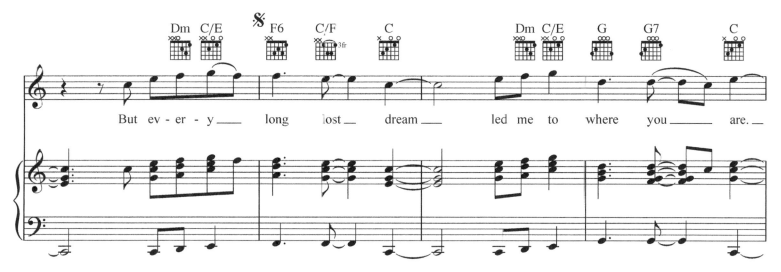

But ev - er - y __ long lost __ dream __ led me to where you __ are. __

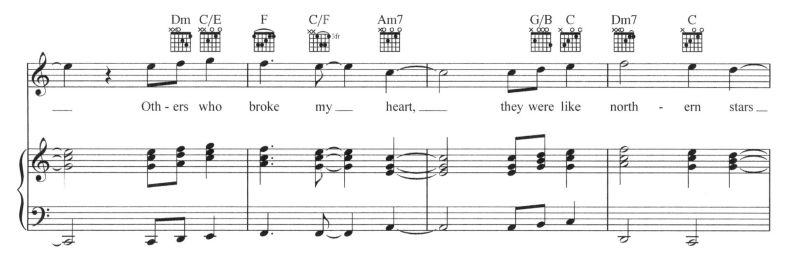

__ Oth - ers who broke my __ heart, __ they were like north - ern stars __

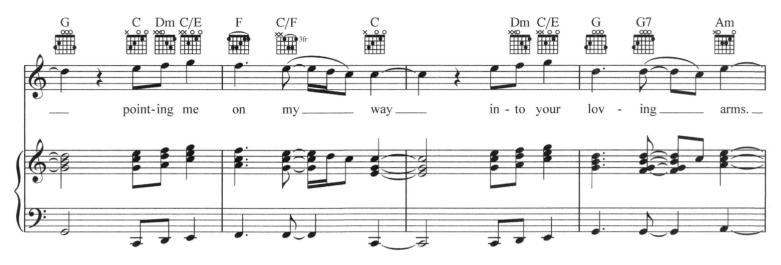

point-ing me on my _____ way _____ in - to your lov - ing _____ arms. _____

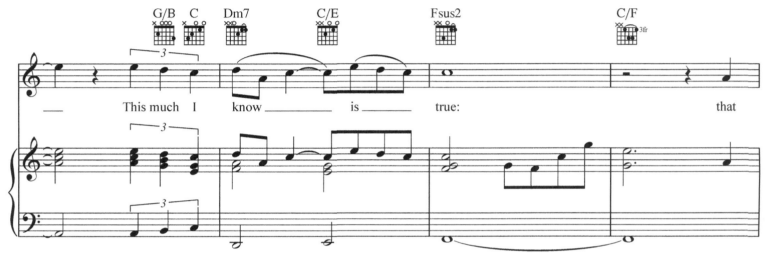

_____ This much I know _____ is _____ true: that

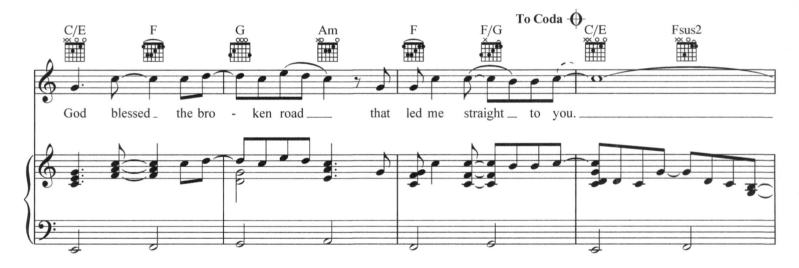

To Coda

God blessed _____ the bro - ken road _____ that led me straight _____ to you. _____

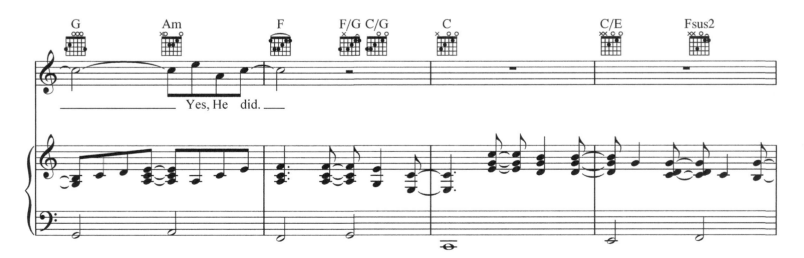

Yes, He did. _____

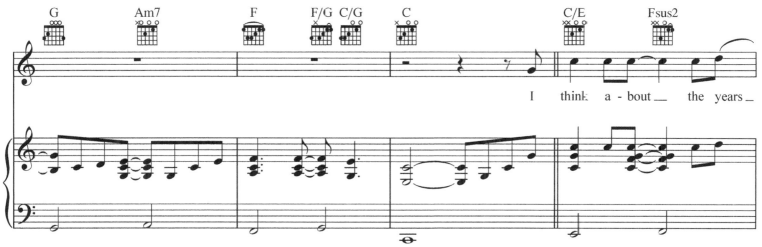

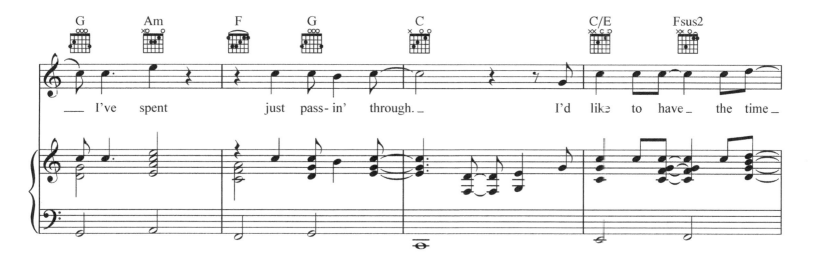

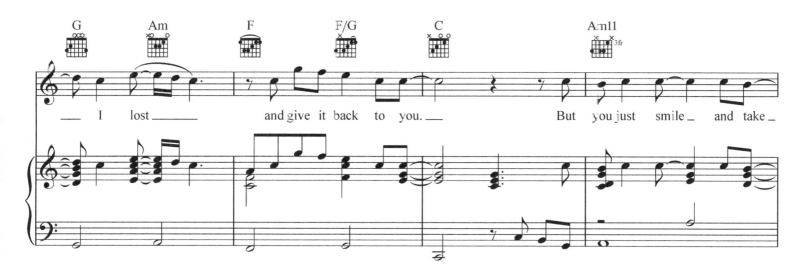

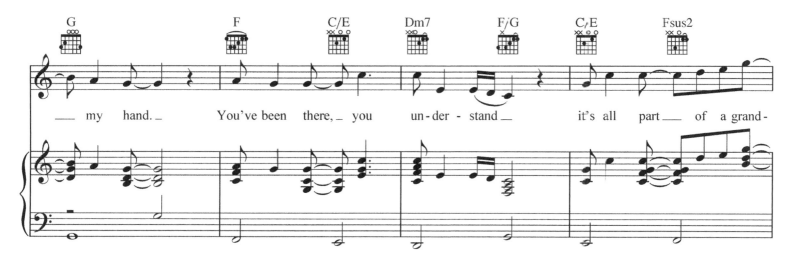

D.S. al Coda

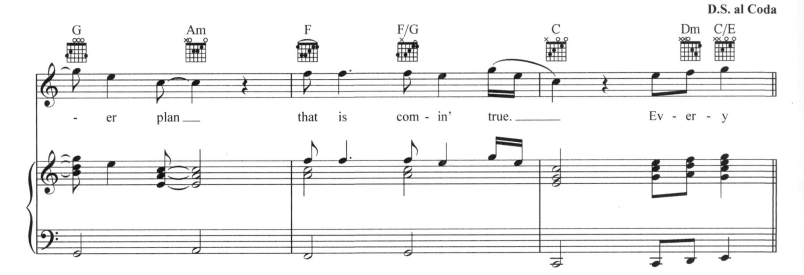

- er plan ___ that is com - in' true. _____ Ev - er - y

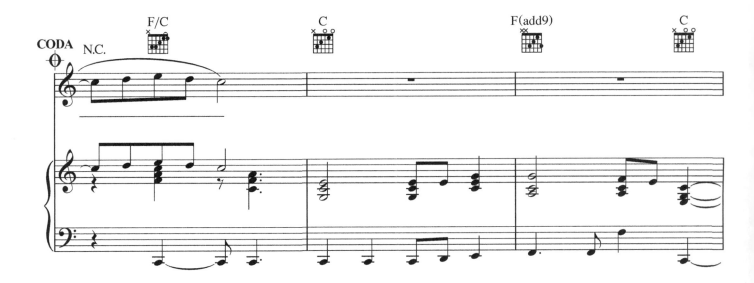

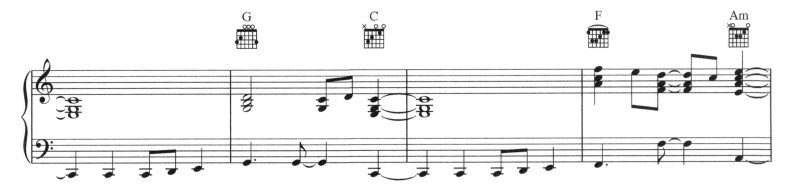

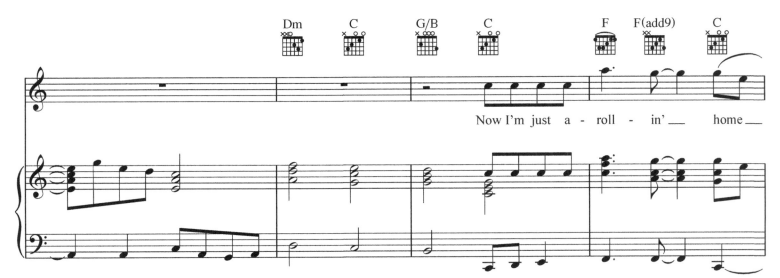

Now I'm just a - roll - in' __ home __

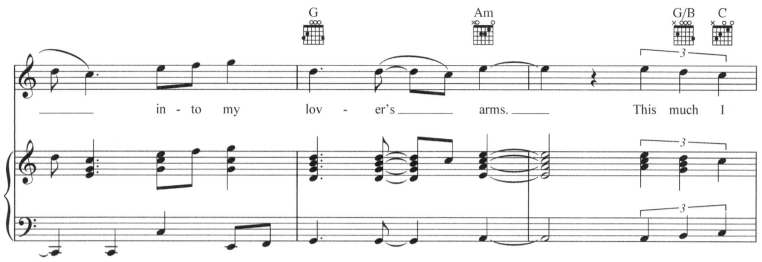

in - to my lov - er's ____ arms. ____ This much I

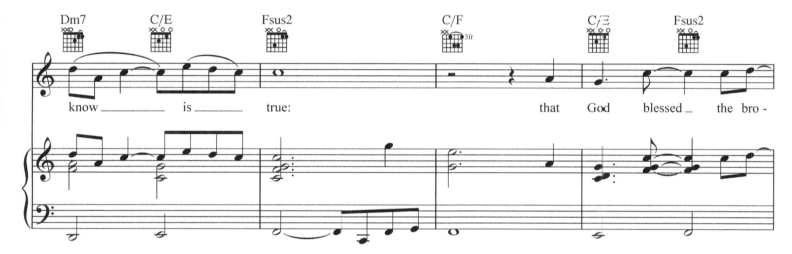

know _____ is _____ true: that God blessed __ the bro -

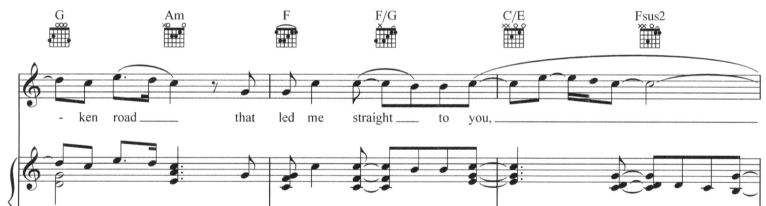

- ken road _____ that led me straight __ to you, _____

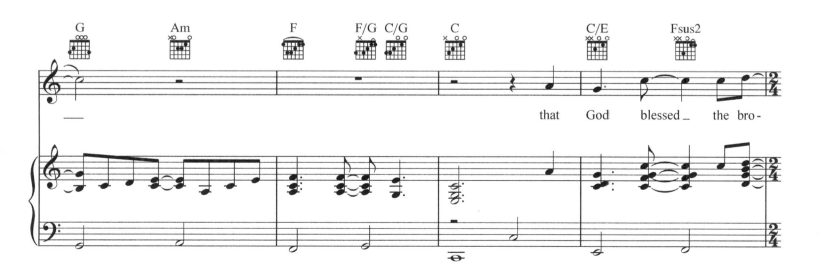

that God blessed __ the bro -

-ken road _____ that led me straight ___

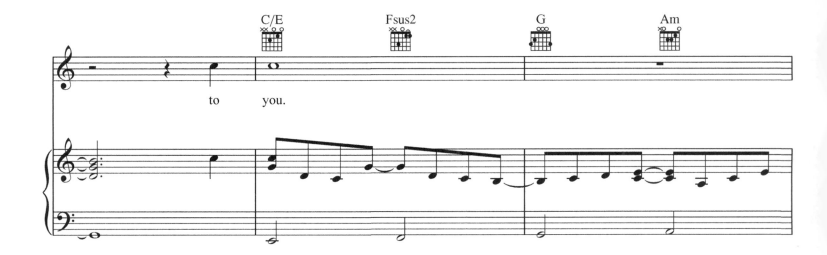

to you.

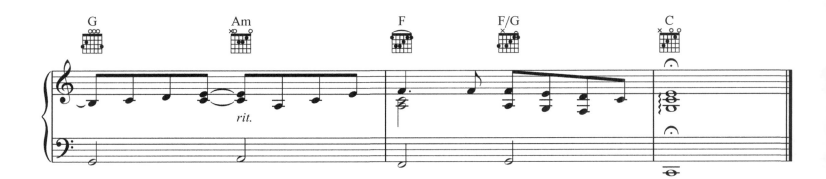

rit.

CANDLE IN THE WIND

Words and Music by ELTON JOHN
and BERNIE TAUPIN

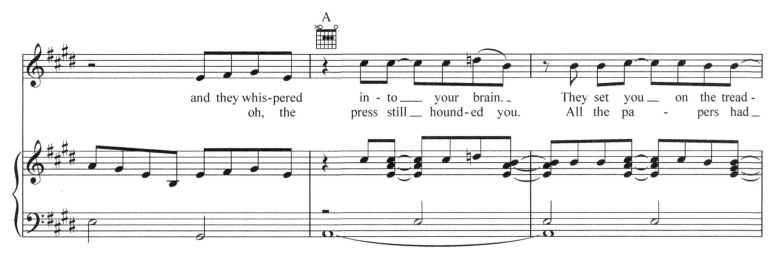

and they whis-pered in - to ___ your brain. They set you ___ on the tread -
oh, the press still ___ hound-ed you. All the pa - pers had ___

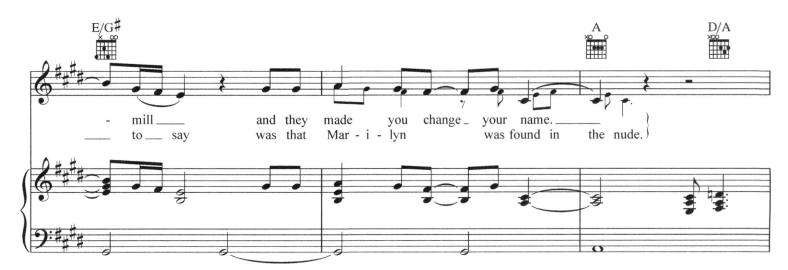

- mill ___ and they made you change ___ your name. ___
___ to ___ say was that Mar - i - lyn was found in the nude.

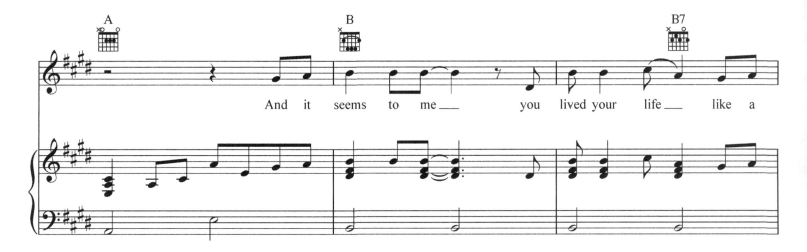

And it seems to me ___ you lived your life ___ like a

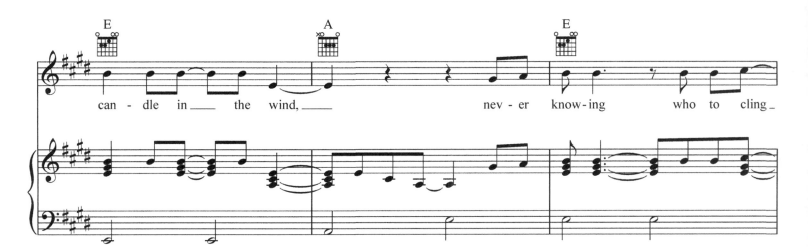

can - dle in ___ the wind, ___ nev - er know-ing who to cling ___

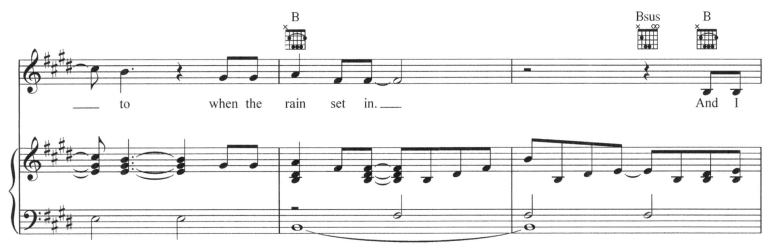

to when the rain set in. ___ And I

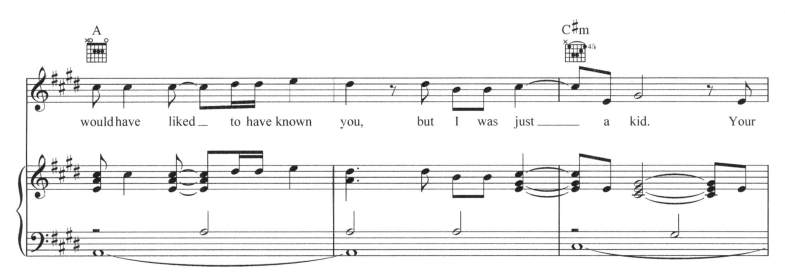

would have liked ___ to have known you, but I was just _____ a kid. Your

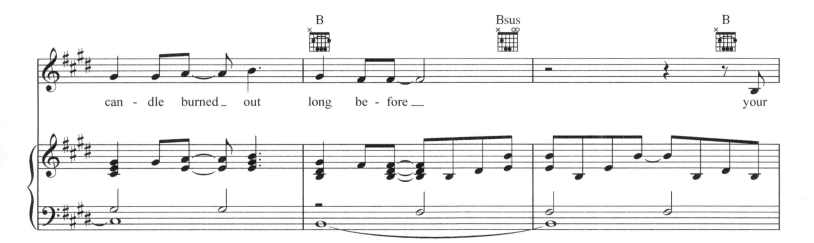

can - dle burned ___ out long be - fore ___ your

leg - end ev - er did. _____

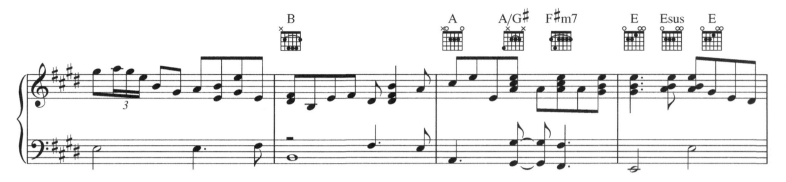

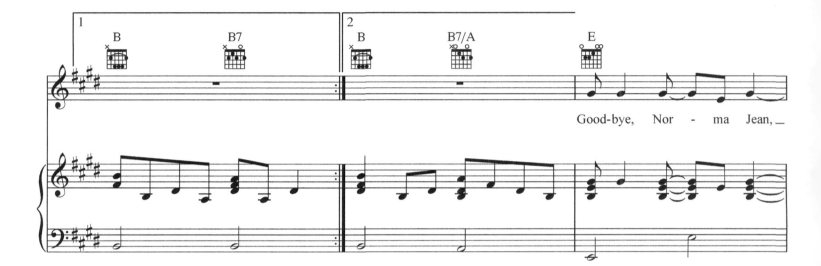

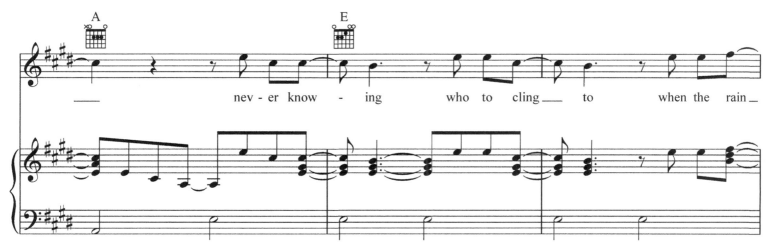

never know - ing who to cling_ to when the rain_

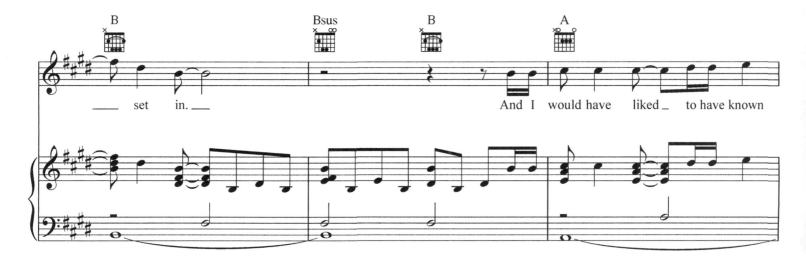

_ set in._ And I would have liked_ to have known

you, but I was just_ a kid. Your can - dle burned_ out

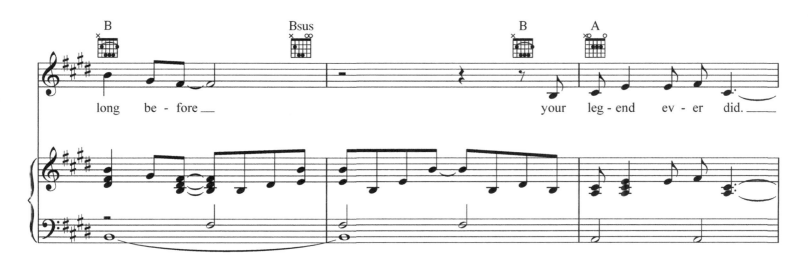

long be - fore_ your leg - end ev - er did._

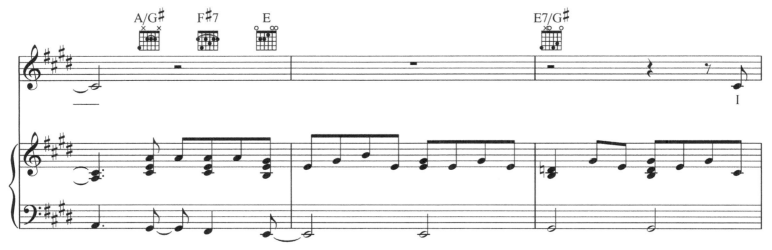

would have liked __ to have known you, whoa, __ but I _____ was just a kid. _____

__ Your can-dle burned __ out long ____ be-fore __

your leg-end ev-er did. _____

rit.

BRIDGE OVER TROUBLED WATER

Words and Music by
PAUL SIMON

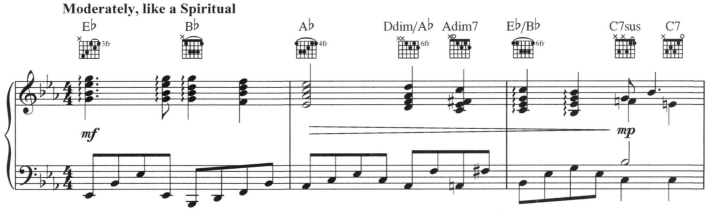

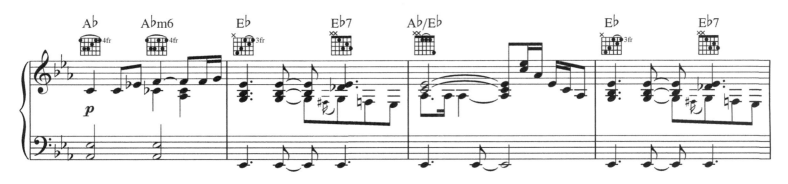

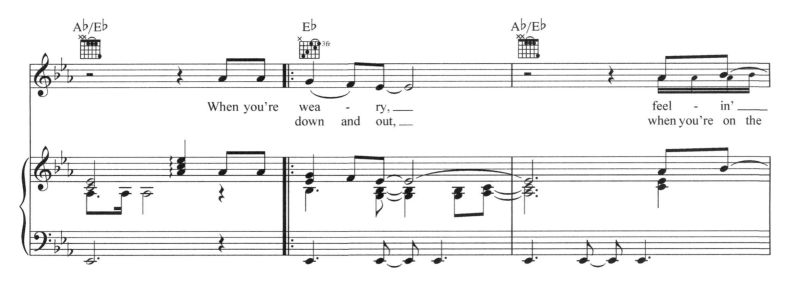

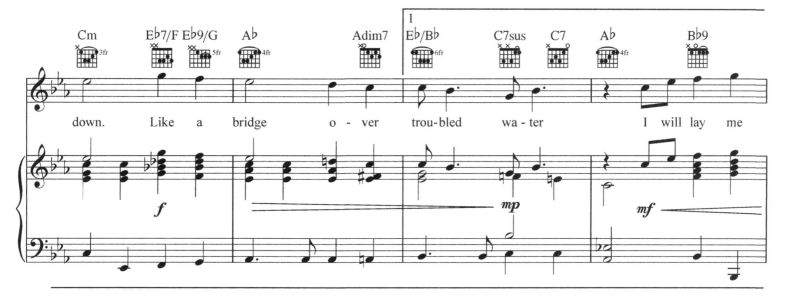

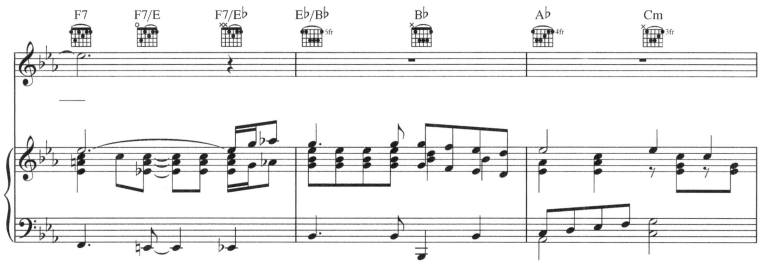

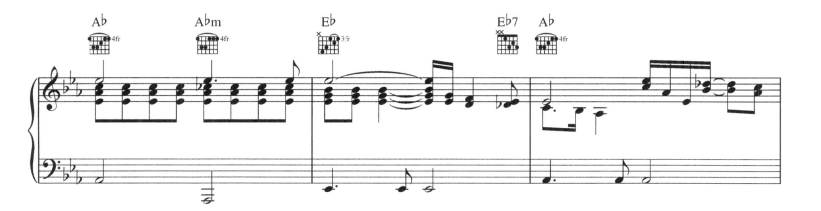

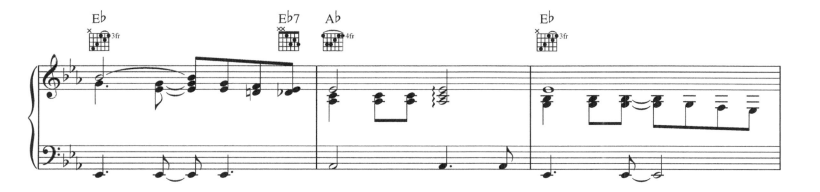

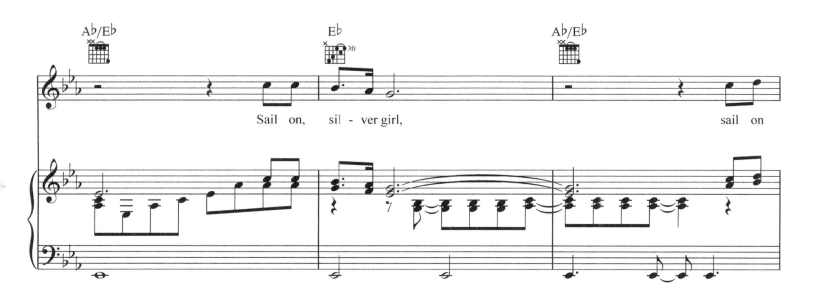

Sail on, sil - ver girl,   sail on

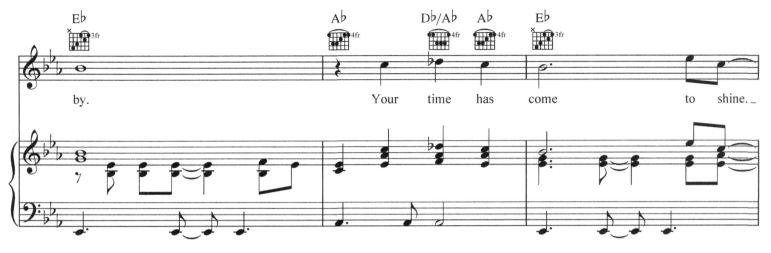

DON'T KNOW MUCH

Words and Music by BARRY MANN,
CYNTHIA WEIL and TOM SNOW

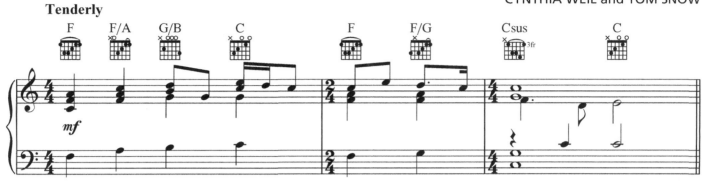

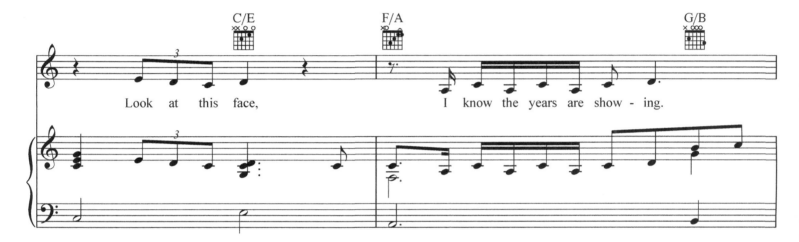

Look at this face, I know the years are show-ing.

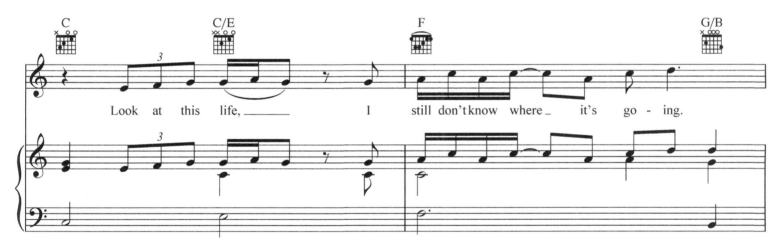

Look at this life, _____ I still don't know where _____ it's go-ing.

I don't know _____ much, but I know I love you, _____ and

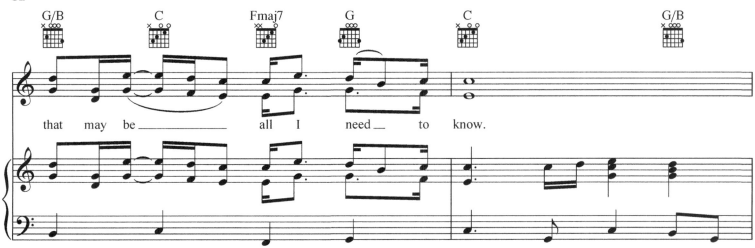

that may be _____ all I need __ to know.

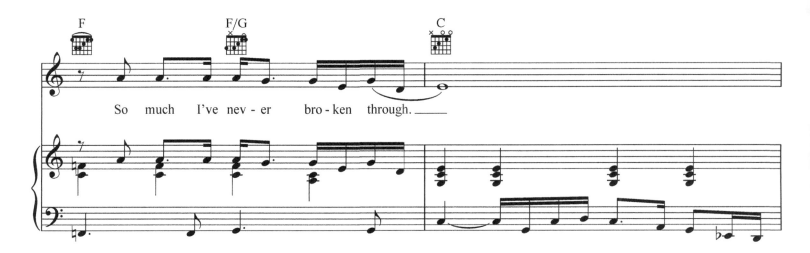

So man - y ques - tions   still left un - an - swered.

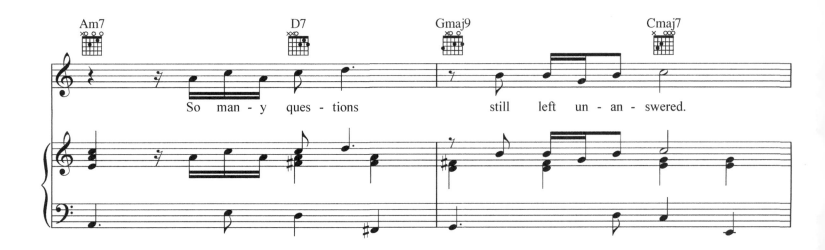

So much I've nev - er bro - ken through. _____

But when I feel you near me,   some-times I see so clear - ly.

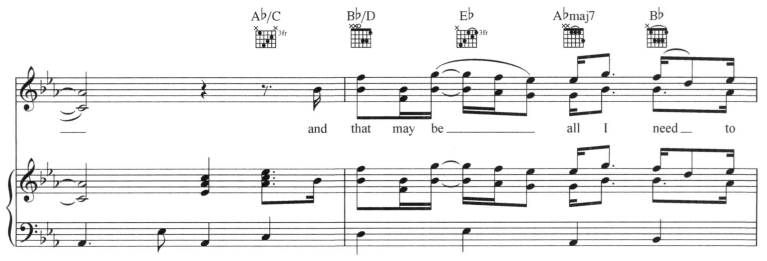

and that may be _____ all I need ___ to

know.

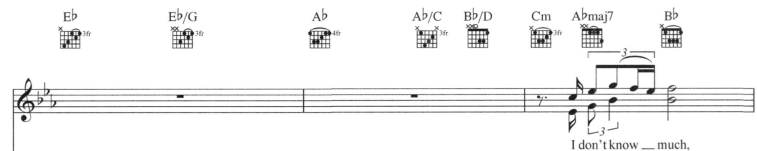

I don't know ___ much,

but I know I love you, _____ and

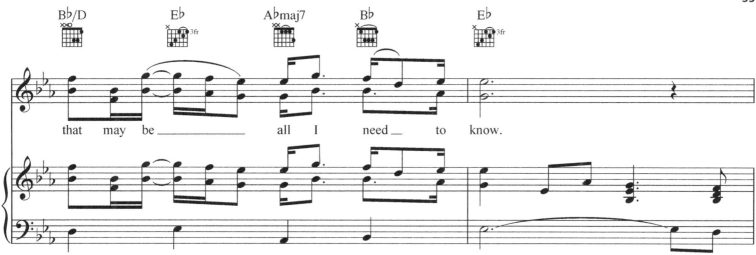

that may be _____ all I need __ to know.

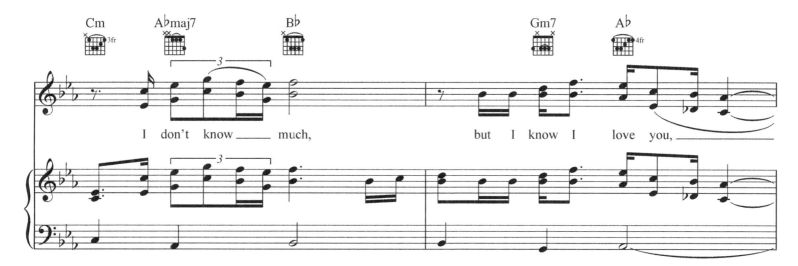

I don't know _____ much, but I know I love you, _____

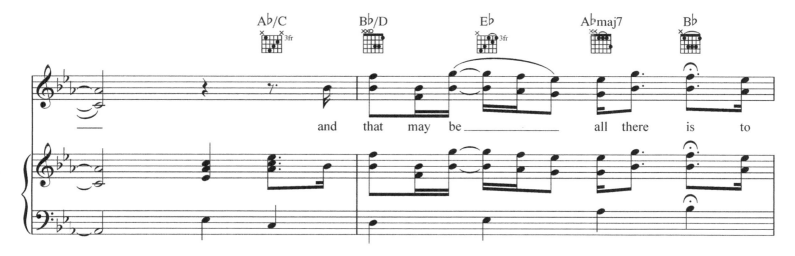

___ and that may be _____ all there is to

know. _____ Whoa. _____

rit.

FIELDS OF GOLD

Music and Lyrics by
STING

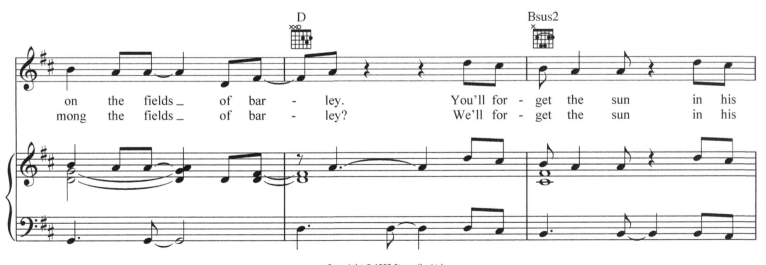

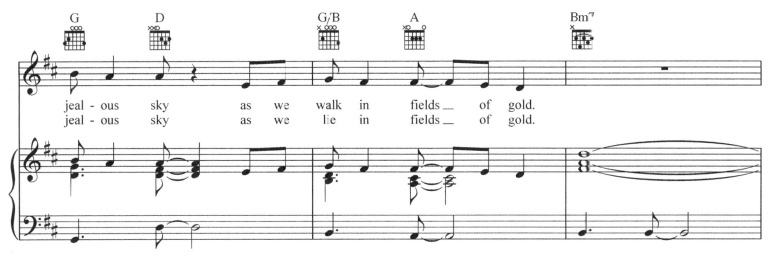

jeal - ous sky   as we   walk in   fields __   of gold.
jeal - ous sky   as we   lie in   fields __   of gold.

So she
See the

took her love   for to   gaze a - while __   up - on   the   fields __   of bar -
west wind move   like a   lov - er so ___   up - on   the   fields __   of bar -

- ley.   In his   arms she fell   as her   hair came   down   a - mong __
- ley.   Feel her   bod - y rise   when you   kiss her   mouth   a - mong __

the fields ___ of gold.
the fields ___ of gold. Will you

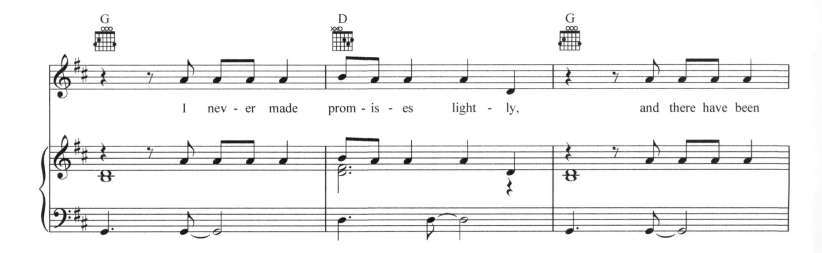

I nev - er made prom - is - es light - ly, and there have been

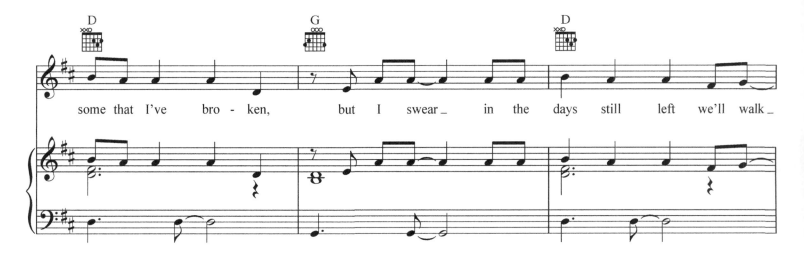

some that I've bro - ken, but I swear ___ in the days still left we'll walk ___

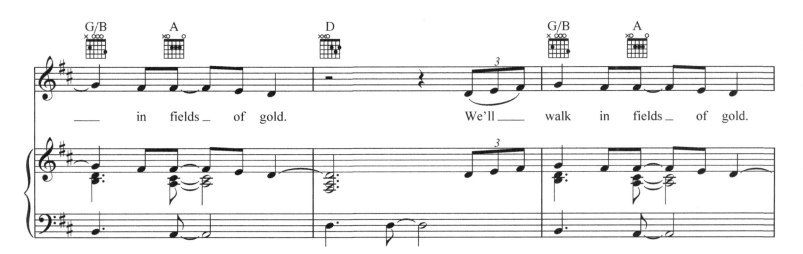

___ in fields ___ of gold. We'll ___ walk in fields ___ of gold.

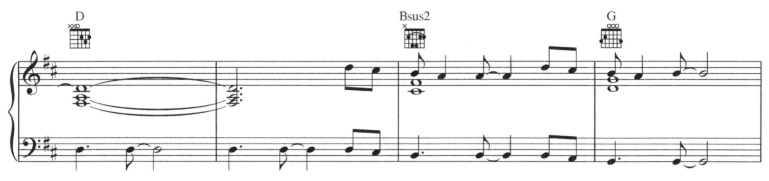

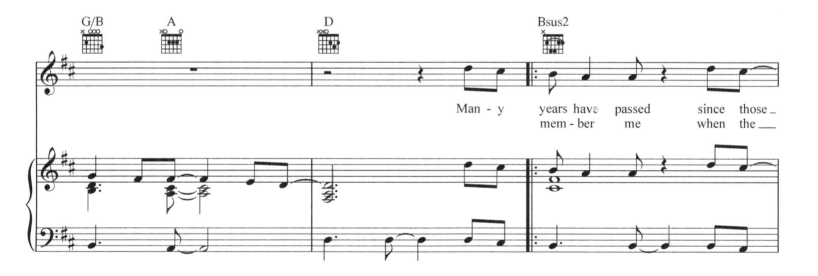

Man - y years have passed since those _
mem - ber me when the _

_ sum - mer days a - mong the fields _ of bar - ley. See the
_ west wind moves up - on the fields _ of bar - ley. You can

chil - dren run as the sun goes down a - mong___ the fields___ of gold.
tell the sun in his jeal - ous sky when we walked in fields___ of gold,

You'll re -

when___ we walked in fields___ of gold,

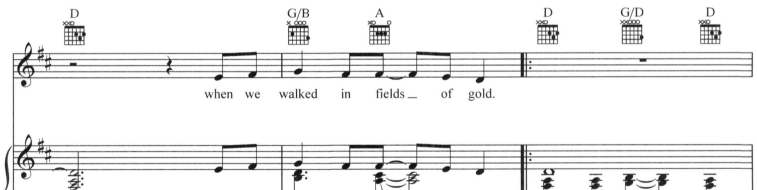

when we walked in fields___ of gold.

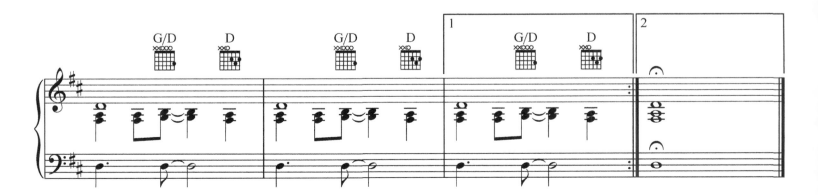

HALLELUJAH

Words and Music by
LEONARD COHEN

FIRE AND RAIN

Words and Music by
JAMES TAYLOR

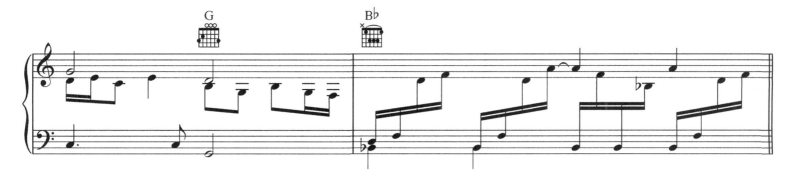

Just yes-ter-day morn-ing they let me know___ you were gone.___
look down up-on me, Je - sus? You got-ta help me make a stand.

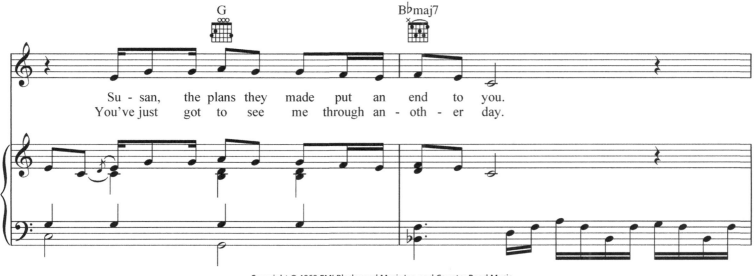

Su - san, the plans they made put an end to you.
You've just got to see me through an - oth - er day.

I walked out this morn - ing and I wrote down this song. __
My bod - y's ach - ing and my time is at hand __

I just can't re - mem - ber who to send __ it to. __
and I __ won't make it an - y oth - er way. __

I've seen fire and I've seen rain.   I've seen

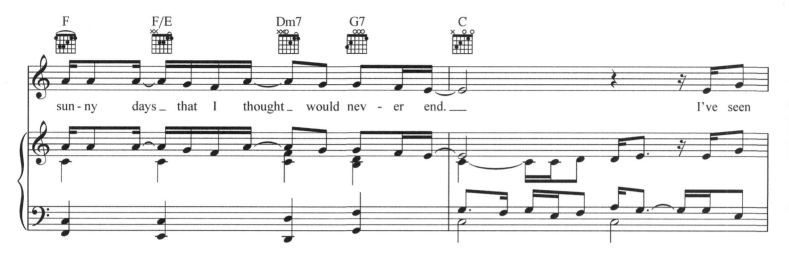

sun - ny days _ that I thought _ would nev - er end. _ I've seen

lone - ly times _ when I could not find a friend, _ but I

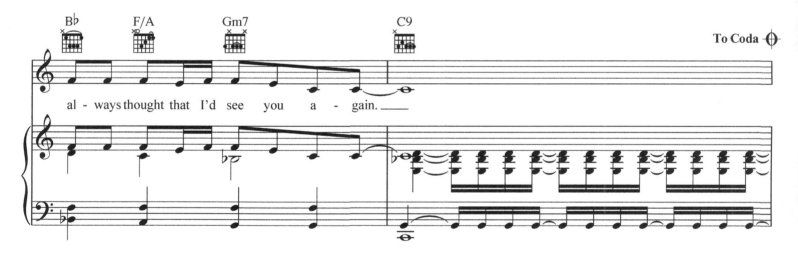

To Coda ⊕

al - ways thought that I'd see you a - gain. _

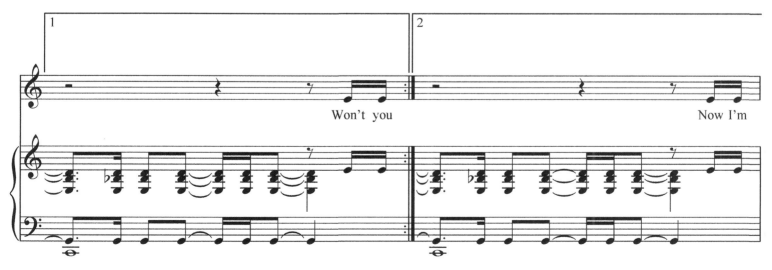

1.

Won't you

2.

Now I'm

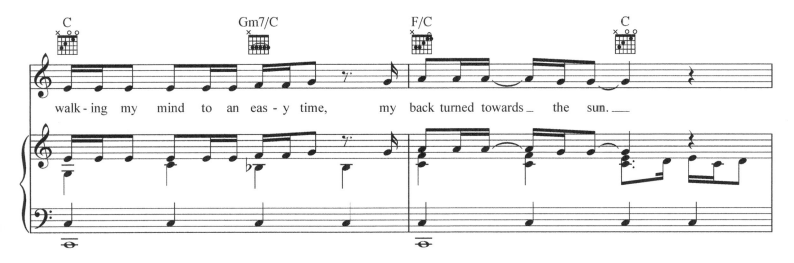

walk-ing my mind to an eas-y time, my back turned towards _ the sun. ___

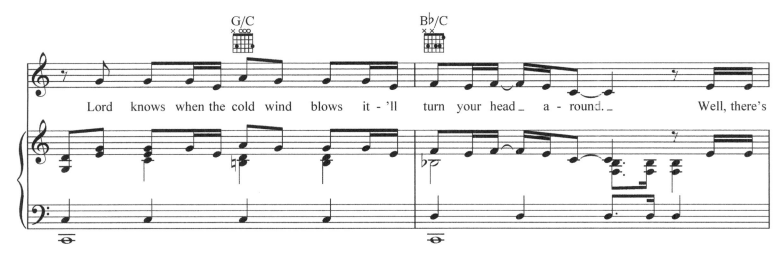

Lord knows when the cold wind blows it-'ll turn your head _ a - round. _ Well, there's

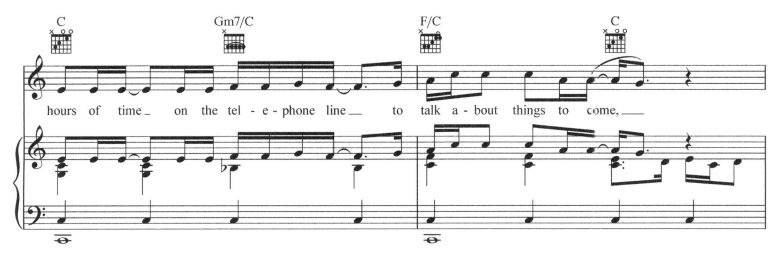

hours of time _ on the tel - e - phone line __ to talk a - bout things to come, ___

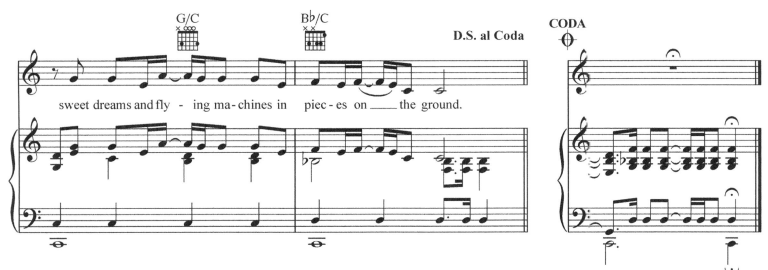

D.S. al Coda

CODA

sweet dreams and fly - ing ma-chines in piec - es on ___ the ground.

HAVE I TOLD YOU LATELY

Words and Music by
VAN MORRISON

Slowly, with expression

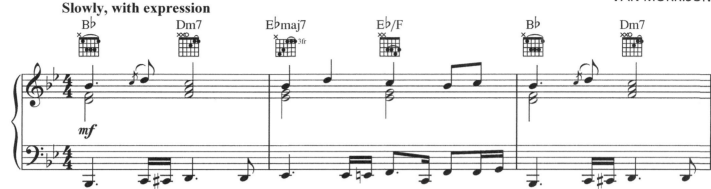

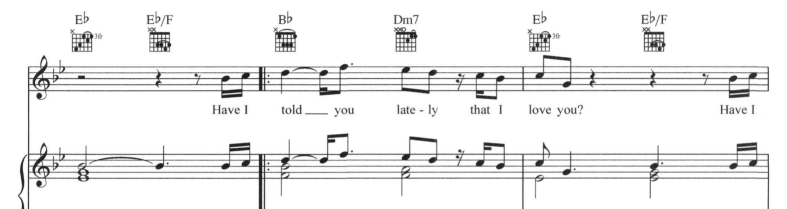

Have I told ___ you late-ly that I love you? Have I

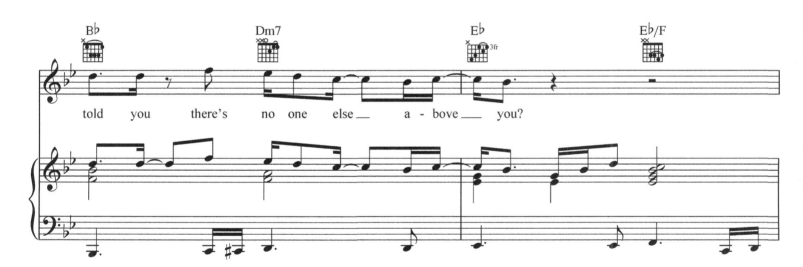

told you there's no one else ___ a-bove ___ you?

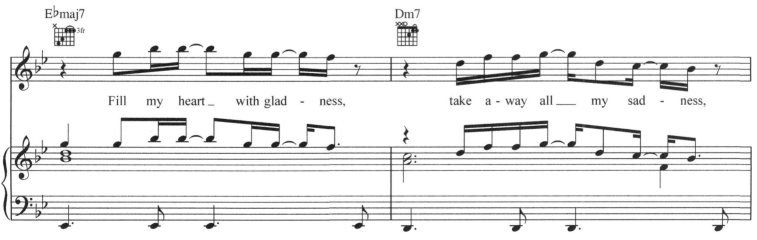

Fill my heart ___ with glad-ness, take a-way all ___ my sad-ness,

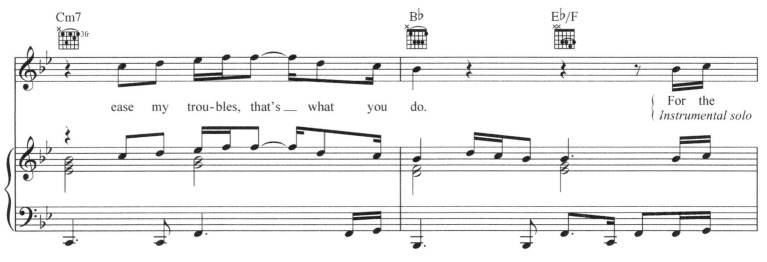

ease my trou-bles, that's __ what you do. For the *Instrumental solo*

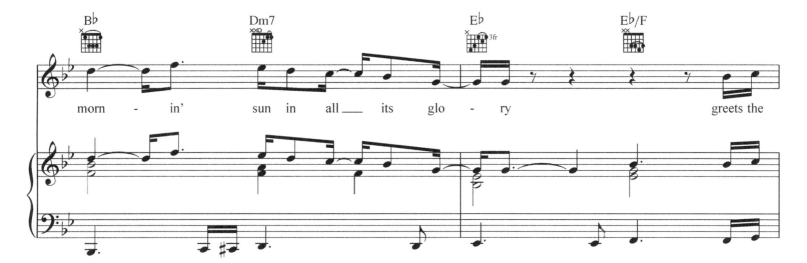

morn - in' sun in all __ its glo - ry greets the

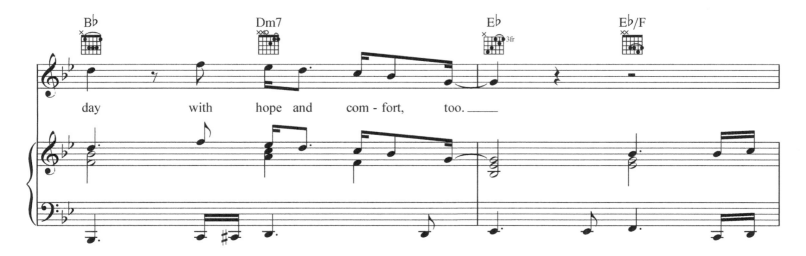

day with hope and com - fort, too. ____

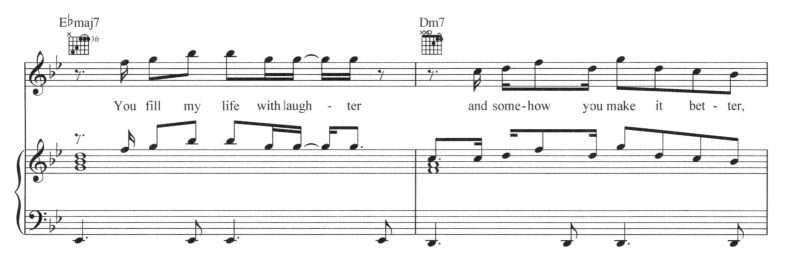

You fill my life with laugh - ter and some-how you make it bet - ter,

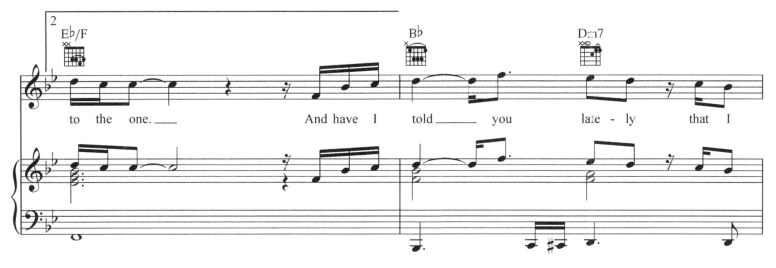

to the one. ___ And have I told ___ you late - ly that I

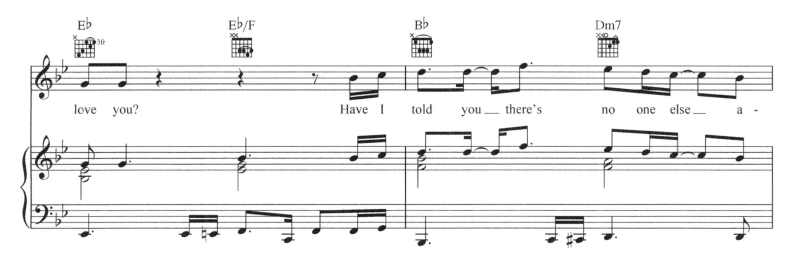

love you? Have I told you ___ there's no one else ___ a -

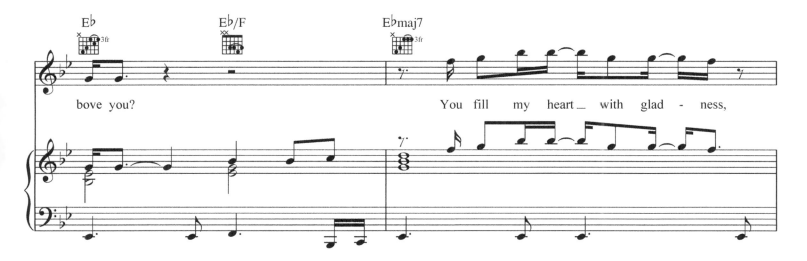

bove you? You fill my heart ___ with glad - ness,

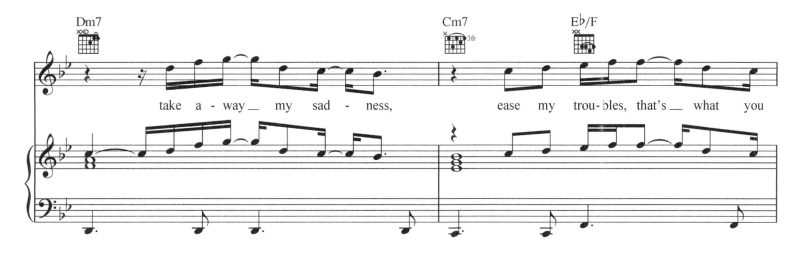

take a - way ___ my sad - ness, ease my trou - bles, that's ___ what you

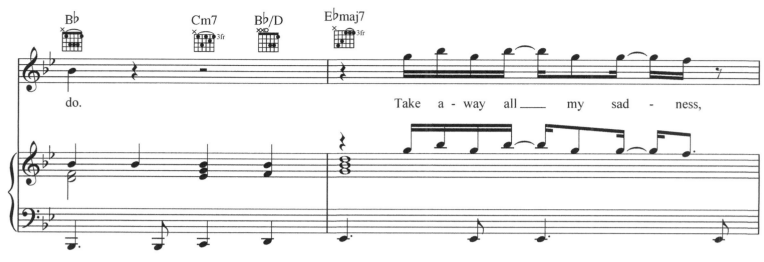

do.

Take a-way all ___ my sad - ness,

fill my life ___ with glad - ness, ease my trou-bles, that's ___ what you do.

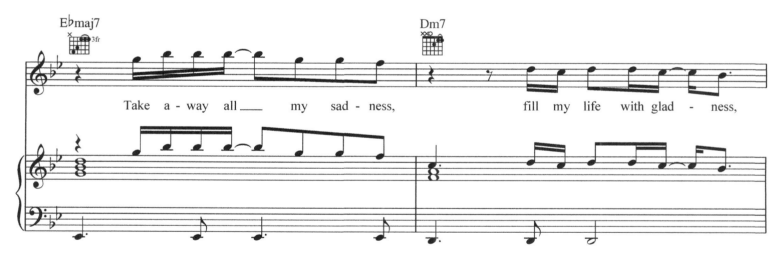

Take a - way all ___ my sad - ness, fill my life with glad - ness,

ease my trou-bles, that's ___ what you do. _____

rall.

(Everything I Do)
I DO IT FOR YOU

from the Motion Picture ROBIN HOOD: PRINCE OF THIEVES

Words and Music by BRYAN ADAMS,
R.J. LANGE and MICHAEL KAMEN

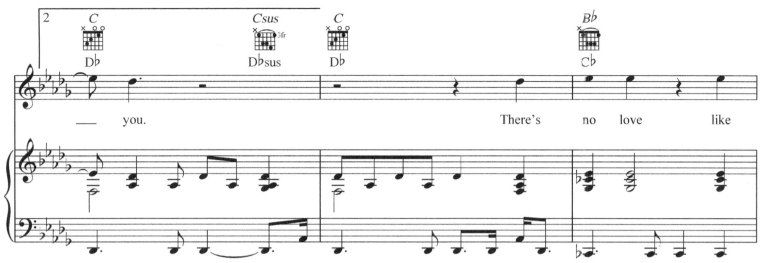

you.

There's no love like

your love, _____ and no oth - er could give

more _____ love. There's no ___ way, _____ un - less

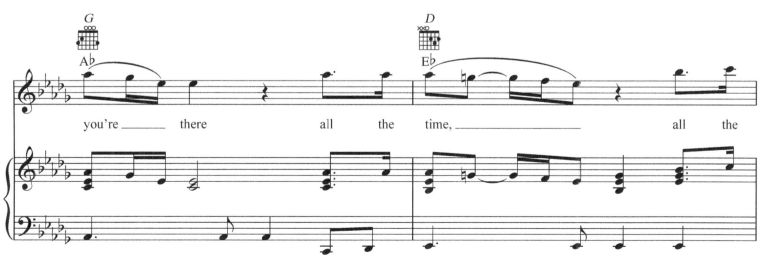

you're _____ there all the time, _____ all the

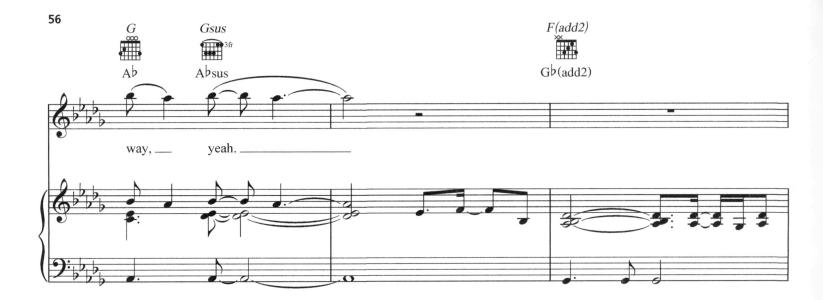

way, ___ yeah. _____

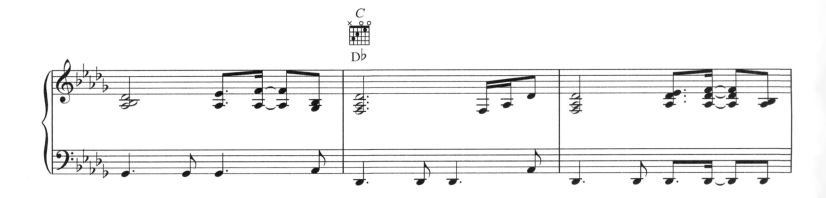

Oh, you can't tell me it's not worth try - ing for. I can't

IMAGINE

Words and Music by
JOHN LENNON

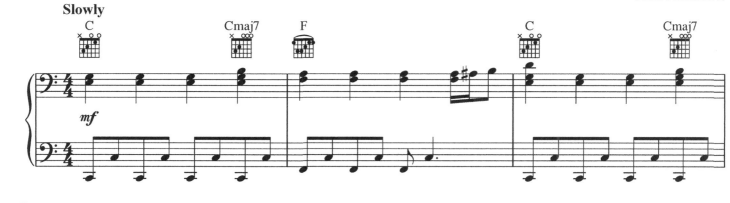

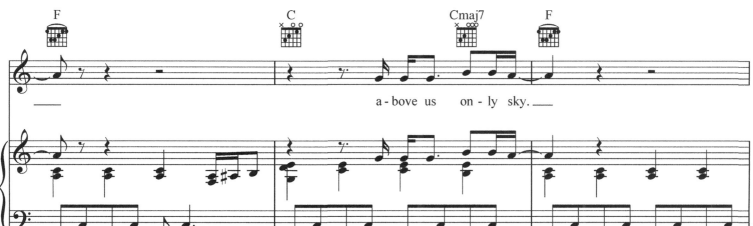

Am/E Dm7 F/C G C/G

I-mag-ine all ___ the peo - ple ___ liv - ing for to - day. __

G7 C Cmaj7 F

Ah. ___ I - mag-ine there's no coun - tries.
sions.

C Cmaj7 F

It is - n't hard ___ to do. ___
I won-der if you ___ can. ___

C Cmaj7 F

Noth-ing to kill ___ or die ___ for,
No need for greed ___ or hun - ger,

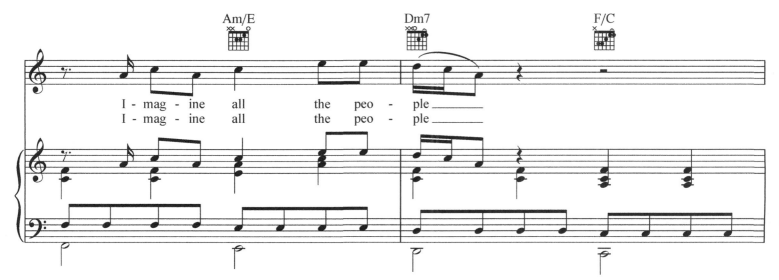

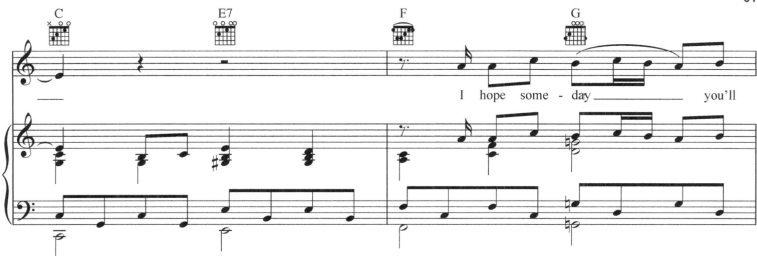

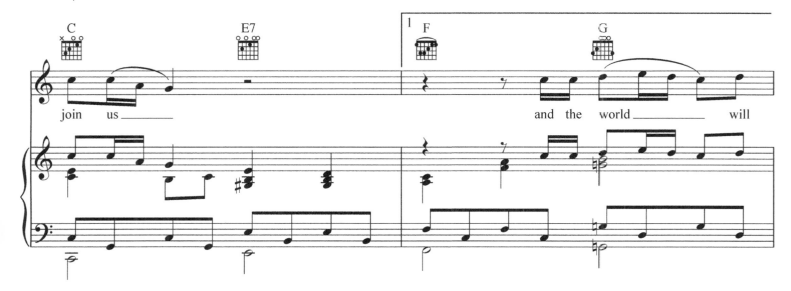

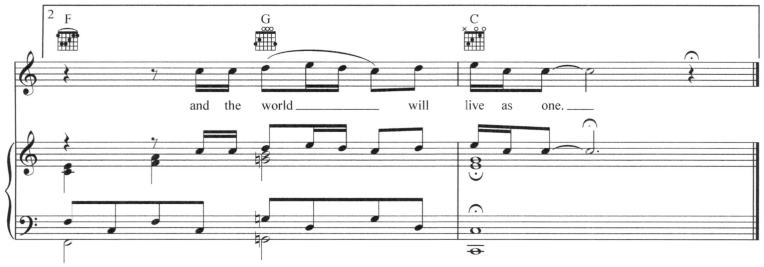

JUST THE WAY YOU ARE

Words and Music by
BILLY JOEL

Moderately

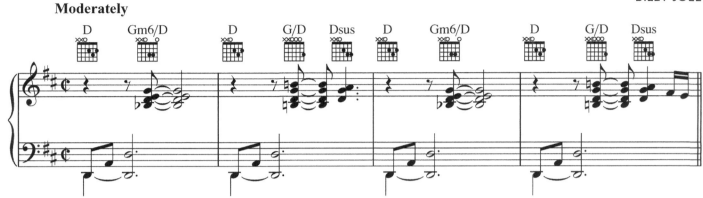

Don't go chang-ing _____ to try and please ___ me. _____

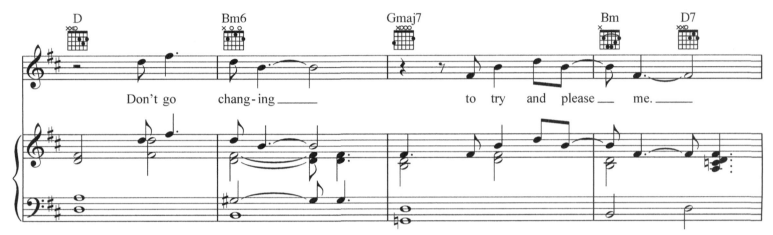

You nev-er let me down ___ be-fore. ___ Mm, _____ mm. ___

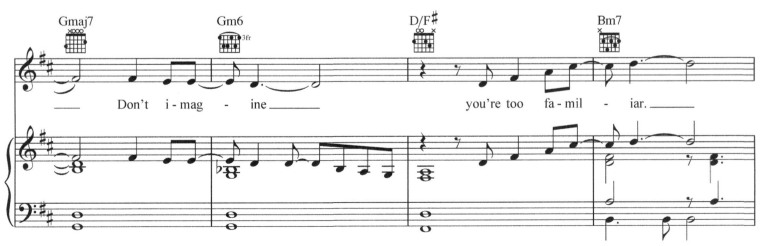

___ Don't i-mag-ine _____ you're too fa-mil-iar. ___

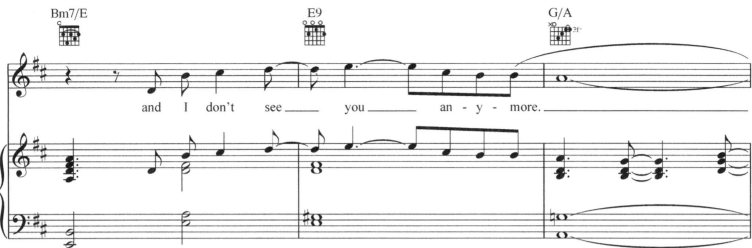

and I don't see ____ you ____ an - y - more. ____

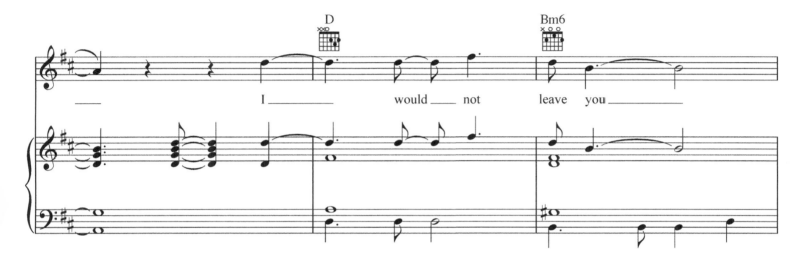

____ I ____ would ____ not leave you ____

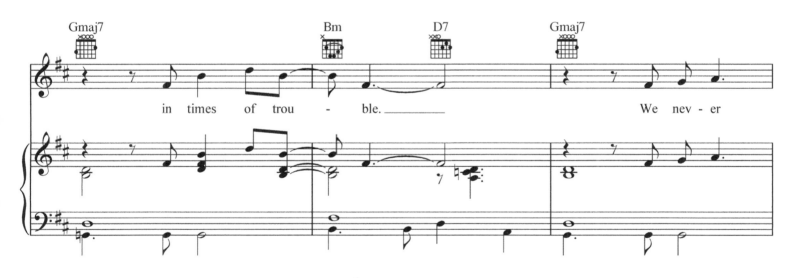

in times of trou - ble. ____ We nev - er

could have come ____ this ____ far. ____ Mm, mm. ____

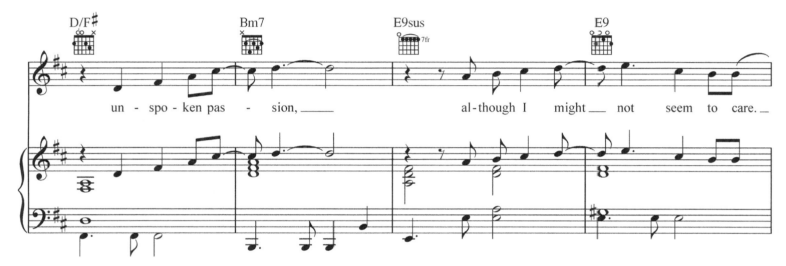

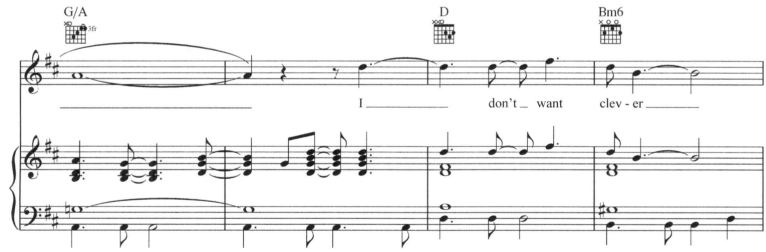

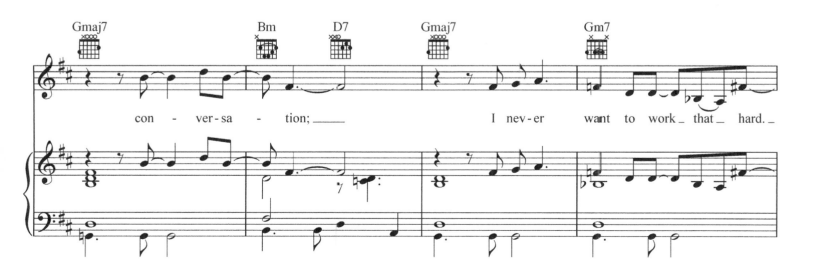

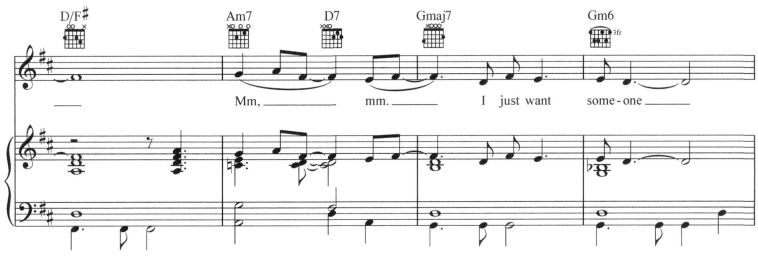

Mm, _____ mm. _____ I just want some-one _____

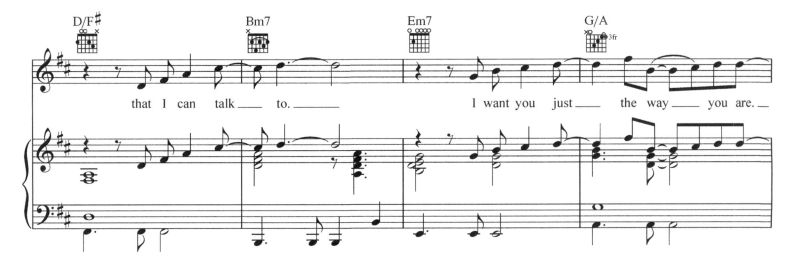

that I can talk ___ to. _____ I want you just ___ the way ___ you are. ___

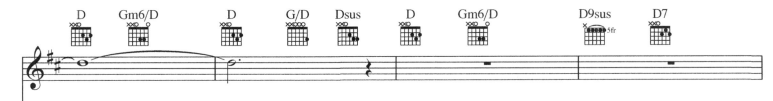

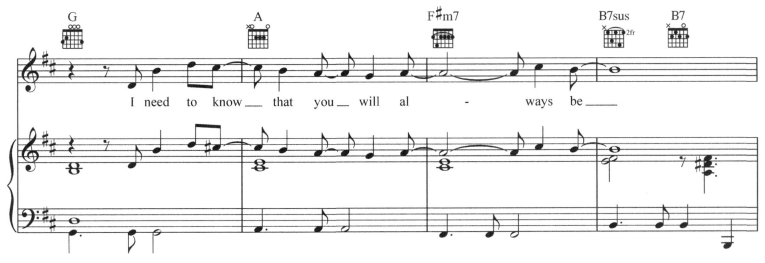

I need to know ___ that you ___ will al - ways be _____

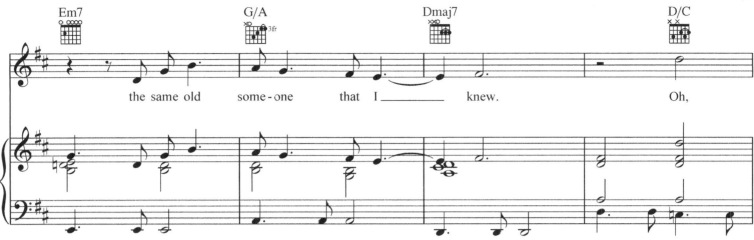

the same old some-one that I _____ knew. Oh,

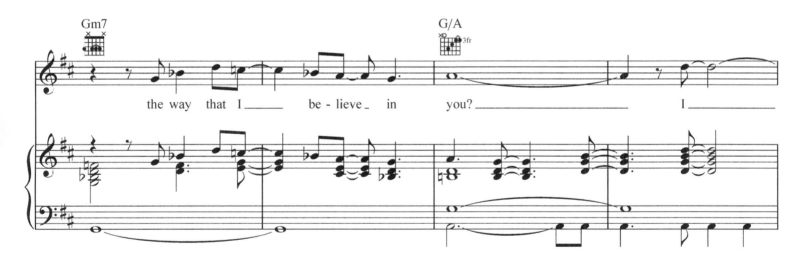

what will it take ___ till you ___ be-lieve _____ in me ___

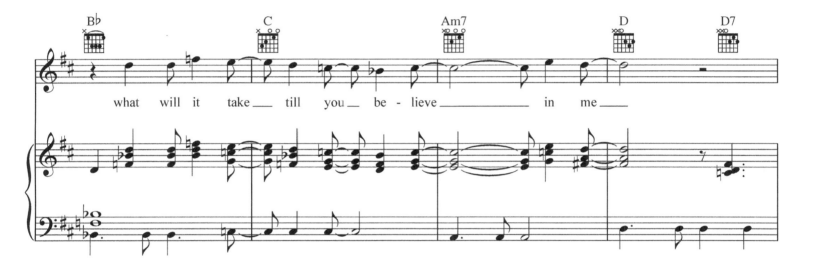

the way that I _____ be-lieve _ in you? _____ I _____

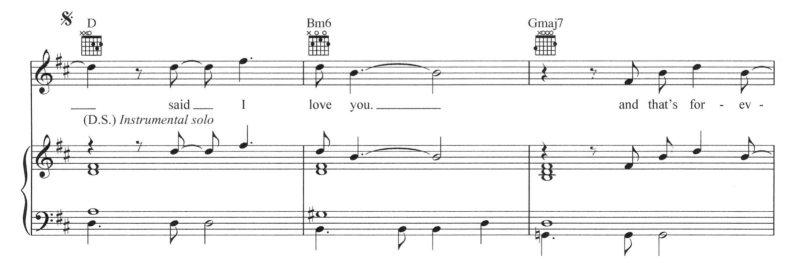

___ said ___ I love you. _____ and that's for - ev -

(D.S.) *Instrumental solo*

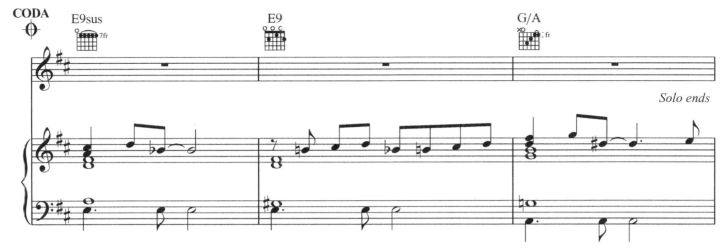

Solo ends

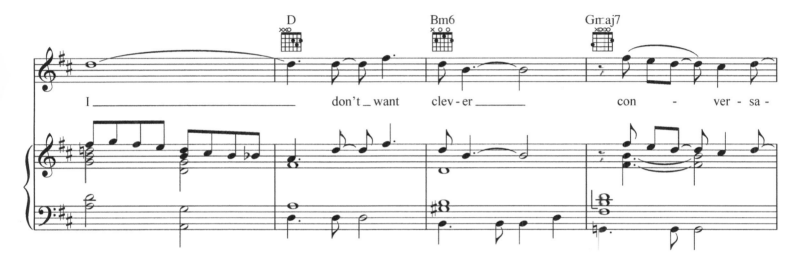

I _____ don't _ want clev-er _____ con - ver-sa-

-tion; I nev-er want _ to work _ that _ hard. _

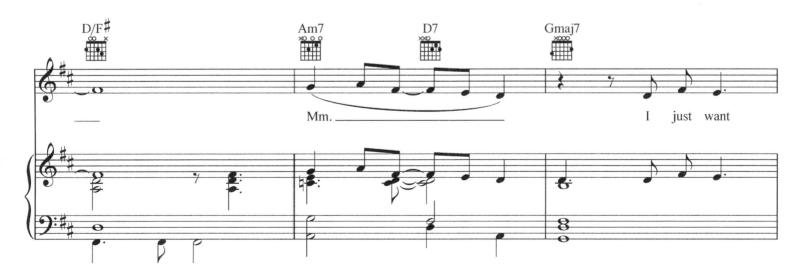

Mm. _____ I just want

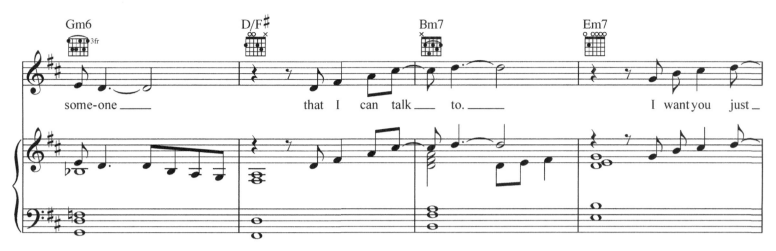

some-one ____ that I can talk ____ to. ____ I want you just ____

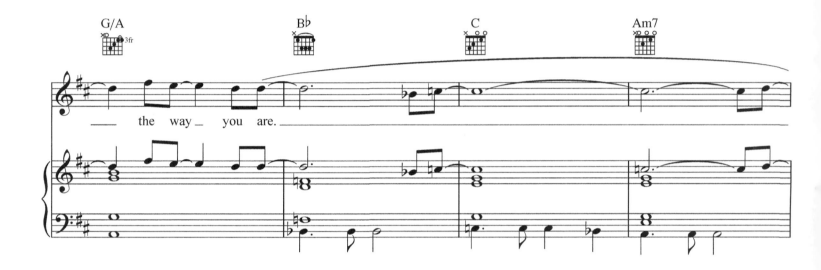

____ the way __ you are. ____

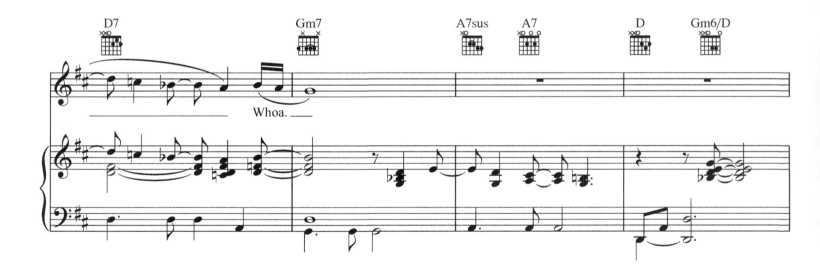

_____ Whoa. ____

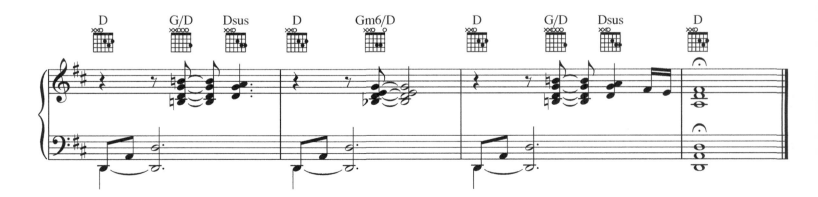

KILLING ME SOFTLY WITH HIS SONG

Words by NORMAN GIMBEL
Music by CHARLES FOX

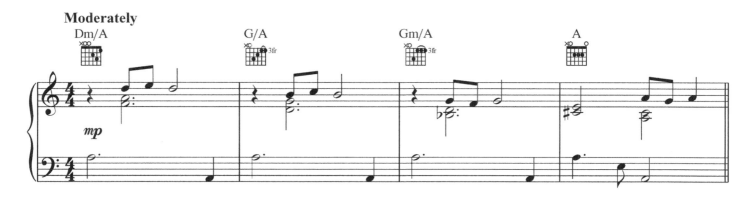

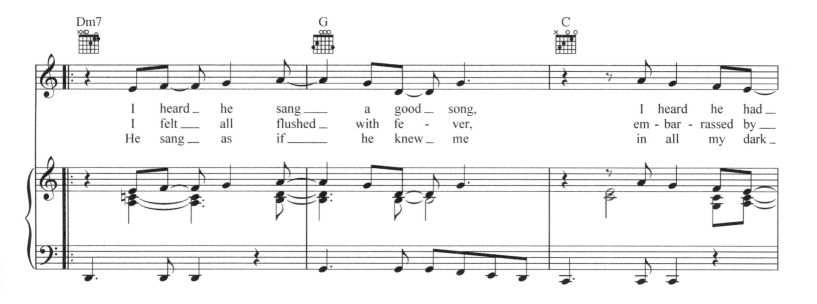

I heard — he sang — a good — song,
I felt — all flushed — with fe - ver,
He sang — as if — he knew — me

I heard he had —
em - bar - rassed by —
in all my dark —

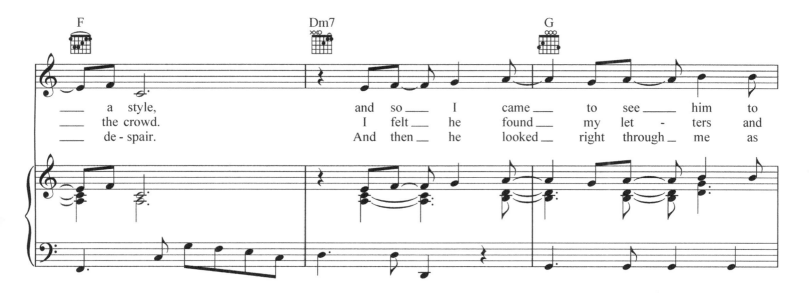

— a style,
— the crowd.
— de - spair.

and so — I came — to see — him to
I felt — he found — my let - ters and
And then — he looked — right through — me as

lis-ten for a - while. _____ And there ___ he was, ___
read each one out loud. _____ I prayed ___ that he ___
if I was-n't there. _____ But he ___ was there, ___

____ this young ___ boy,   a stran - ger to ____ my eyes. ____
would fin - ish,   but he just kept ___ right on. ____
____ this stran - ger,   sing - ing clear ___ and strong. ____

Strum-ming my pain ___ with his fin - gers, ____ sing-ing my life ___ with his words. _

Kill-ing me soft - ly with his ___ song, kill-ing me soft-

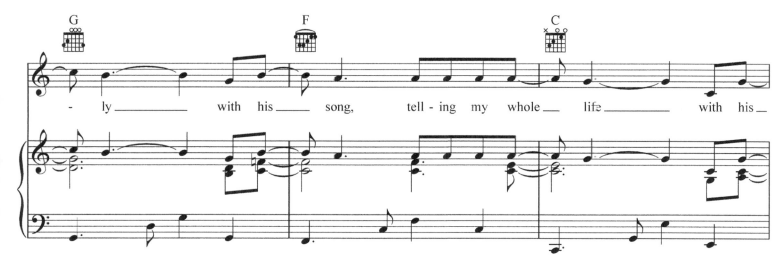

- ly _____ with his ___ song, tell-ing my whole ___ life _____ with his ___

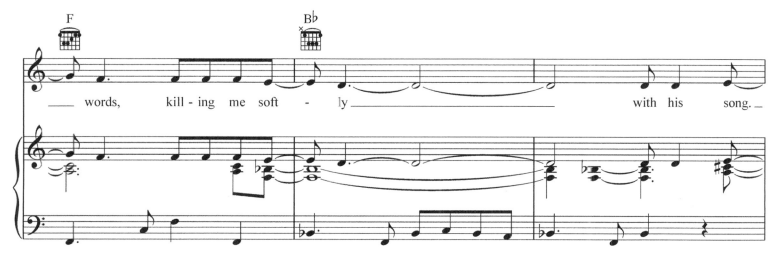

___ words, kill-ing me soft - ly _____ with his song. ___

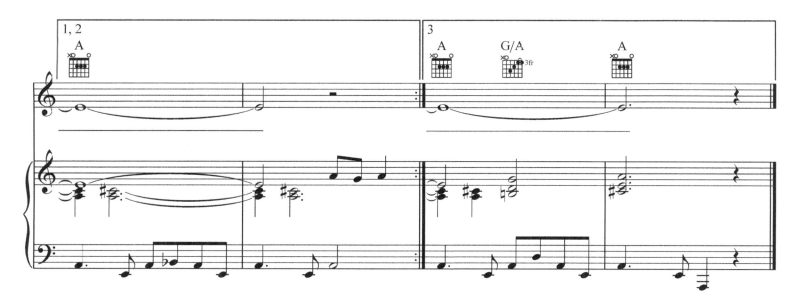

THE LONG AND WINDING ROAD

Words and Music by JOHN LENNON
and PAUL McCARTNEY

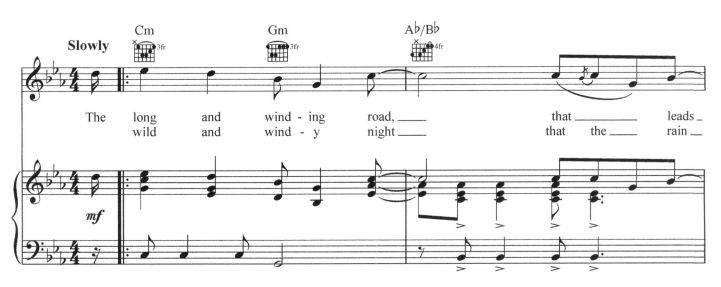

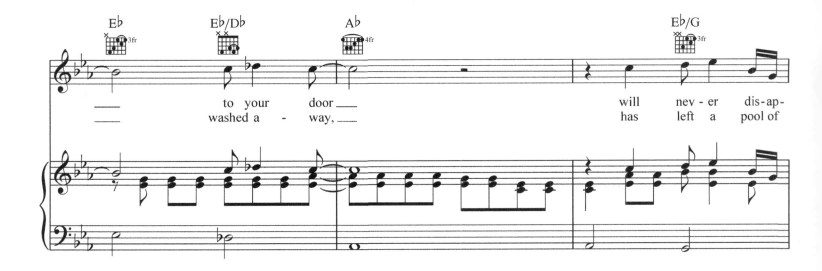

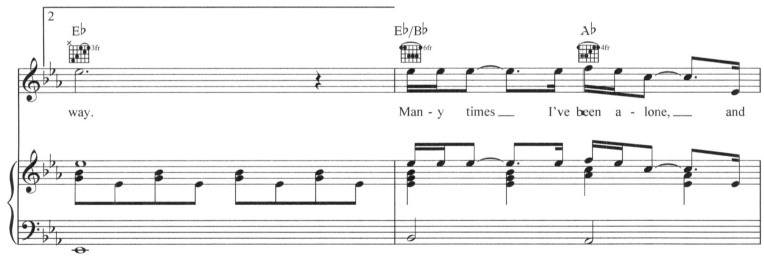

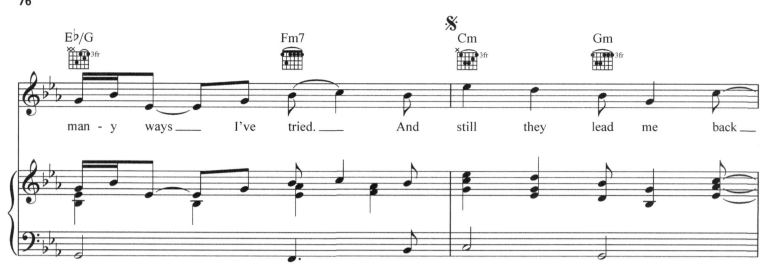

man - y ways ___ I've tried. ___ And still they lead me back ___

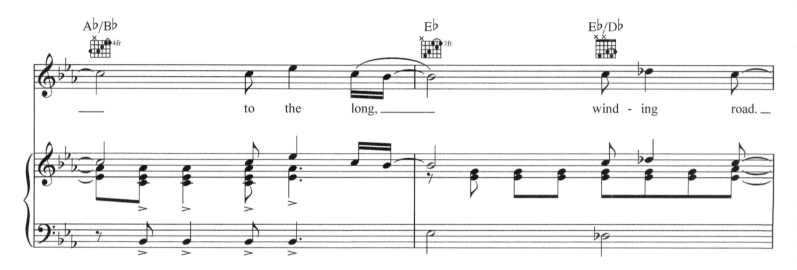

___ to the long, _____ wind - ing road. __

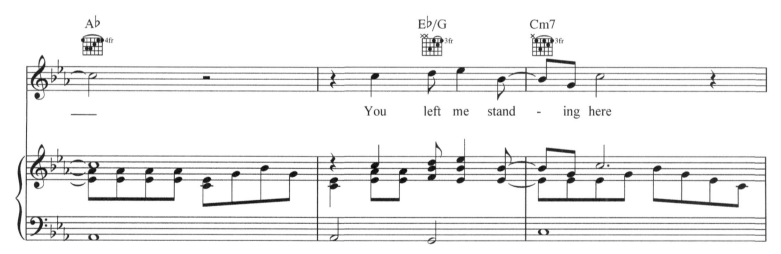

___ You left me stand - ing here

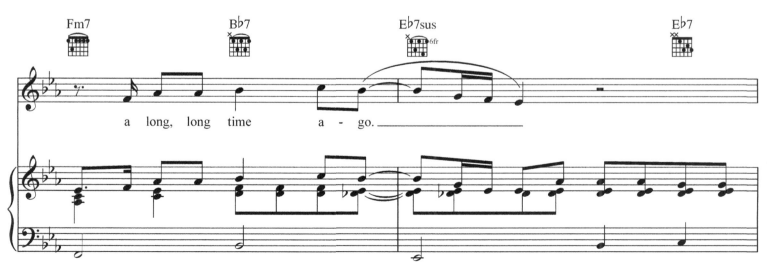

a long, long time a - go. _____

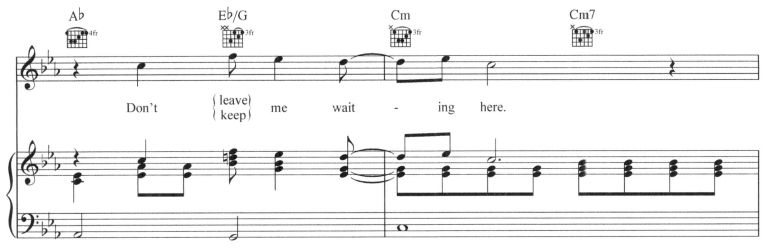

Don't {leave}{keep} me wait - ing here.

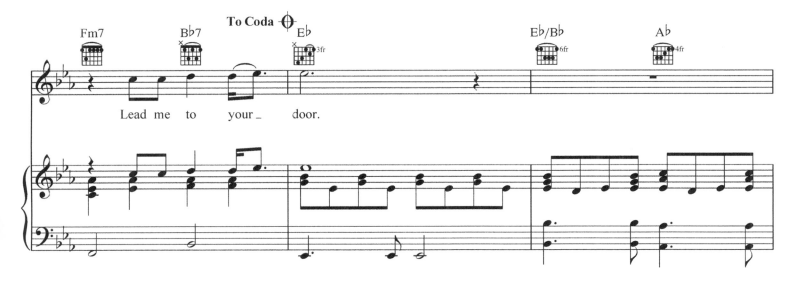

Lead me to your _ door.

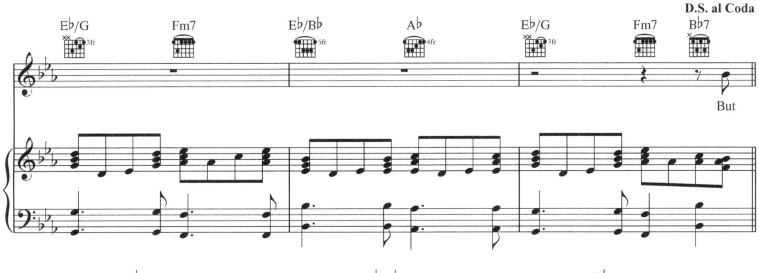

But

door.   Yeah, yeah, yeah,   yeah. ___

MORE THAN WORDS

Words and Music by NUNO BETTENCOURT
and GARY CHERONE

Moderately slow

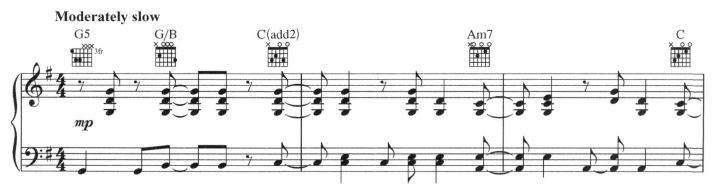

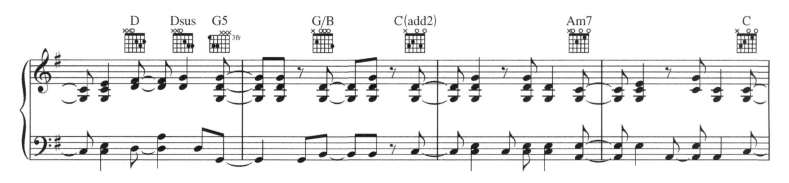

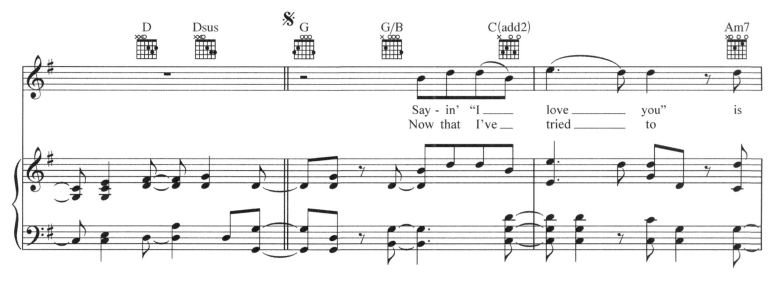

Say - in' "I ___ love ___ you" is
Now that I've ___ tried ___ to

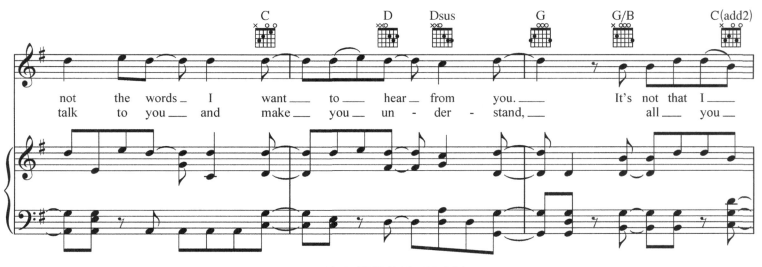

not the words ___ I want ___ to ___ hear ___ from you. ___ It's not that I ___
talk to you ___ and make ___ you ___ un - der - stand, ___ all ___ you ___

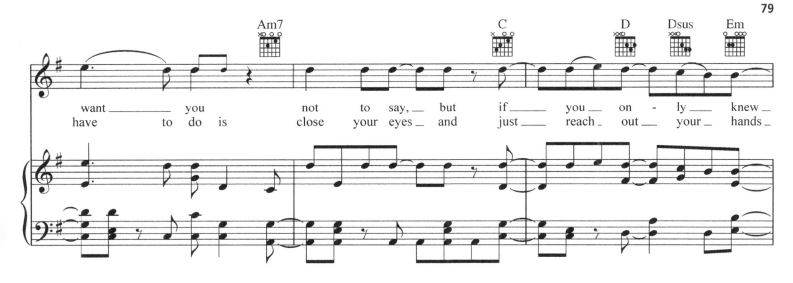

want _____ you _____ not _____ to say, _____ but _____ if _____ you _____ on - ly _____ knew _____
have _____ to do is _____ close _____ your eyes _____ and _____ just _____ reach _____ out _____ your _____ hands _____

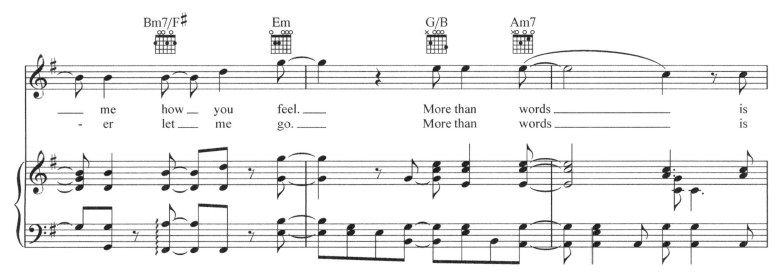

_____ how _____ eas - y _____ it would be _____ to _____ show _____
_____ and _____ touch me. _____ Hold me close _____ don't _____ ev -

_____ me how _____ you _____ feel. _____ More than _____ words _____ is
- er _____ let _____ me _____ go. _____ More than _____ words _____ is

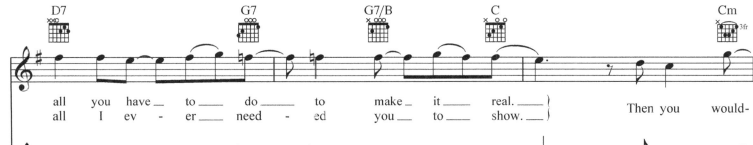

all you have _____ to _____ do _____ to _____ make _____ it _____ real. _____
all I ev - er _____ need - ed _____ you _____ to _____ show. _____

Then you would-

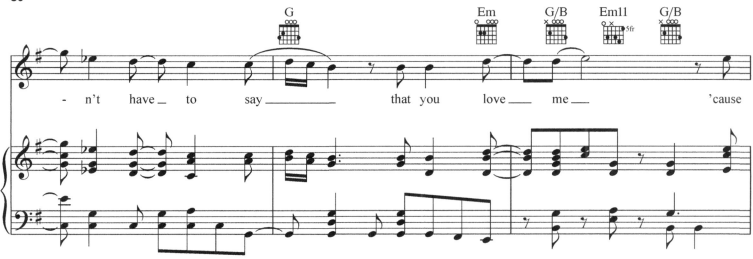

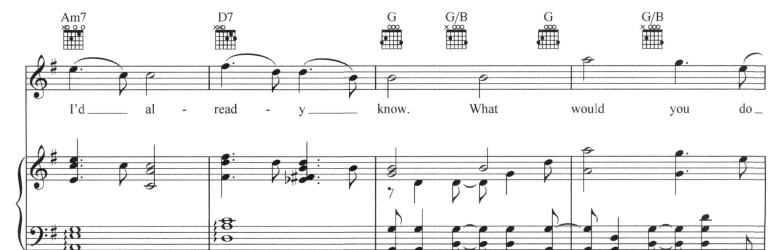

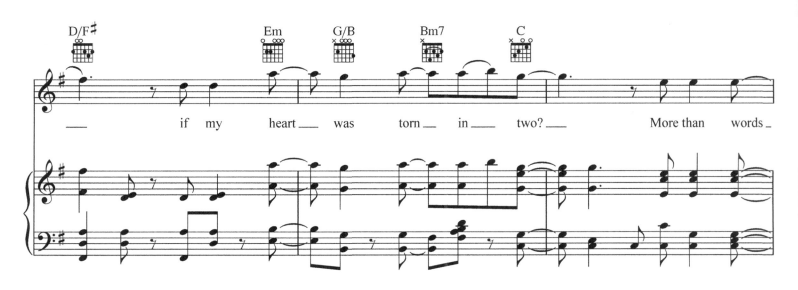

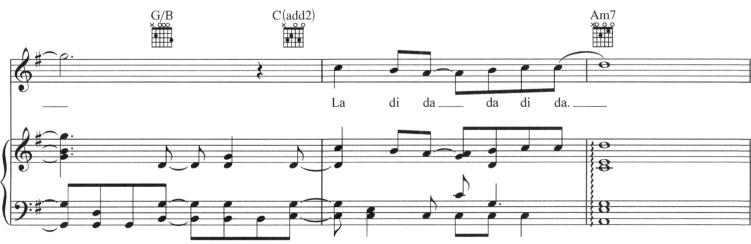

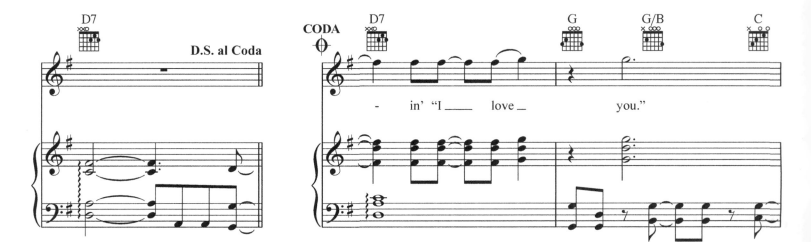

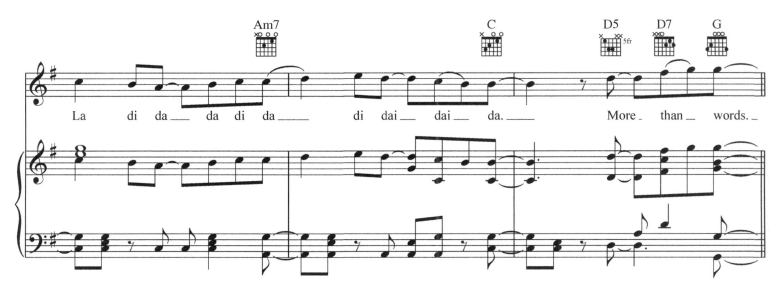

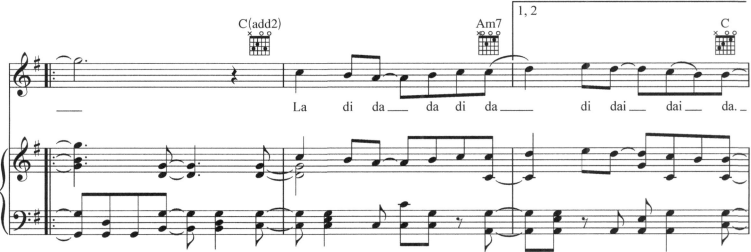

MY HEART WILL GO ON

(Love Theme from 'Titanic')

from the Paramount and Twentieth Century Fox Motion Picture TITANIC

Music by JAMES HORNER
Lyric by WILL JENNINGS

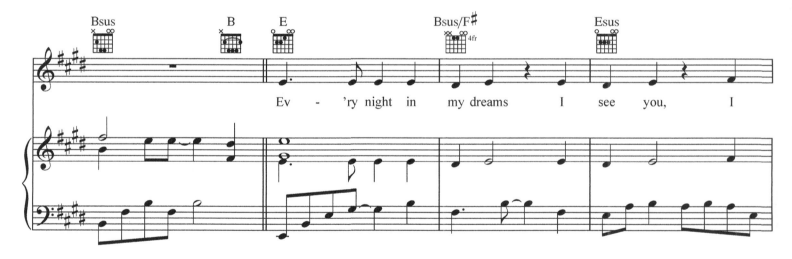

Ev - 'ry night in my dreams I see you, I

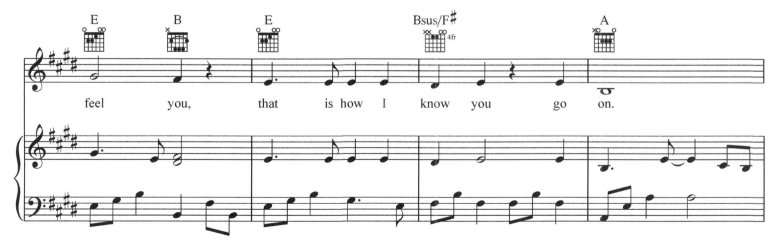

feel you, that is how I know you go on.

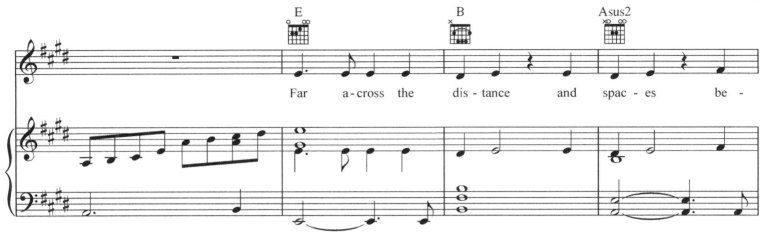

Far a-cross the dis-tance and spac-es be -

tween us, you have come to show you go on.

Near, far, wher-ev - er you are, _

_____ I be - lieve that the heart does go on. _____

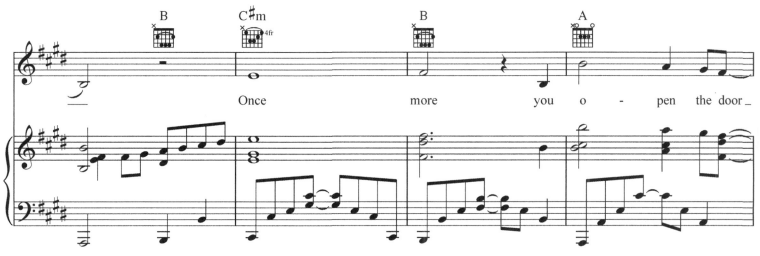

Once more you o - pen the door _

_ and you're here in my heart, and my heart will go

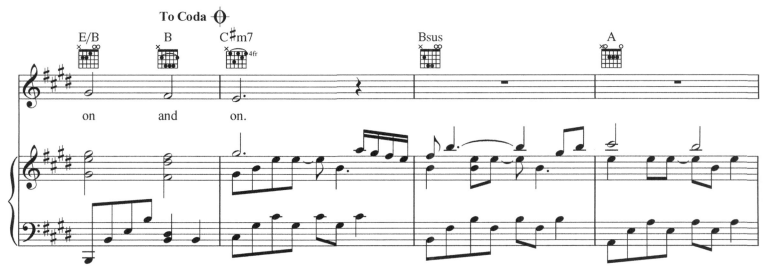

To Coda

on and on.

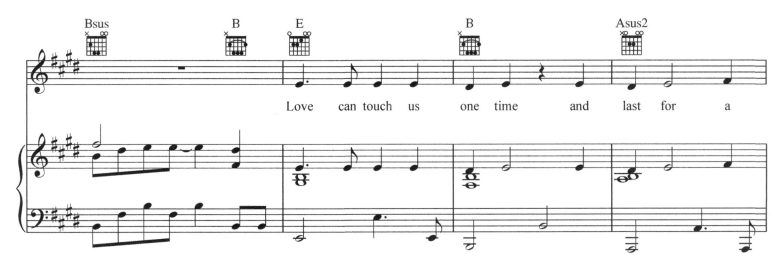

Love can touch us one time and last for a

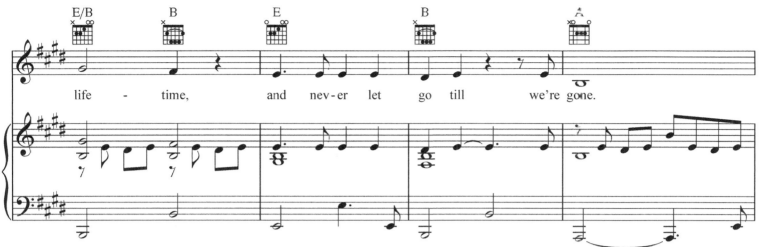

life - time, and nev-er let go till we're gone.

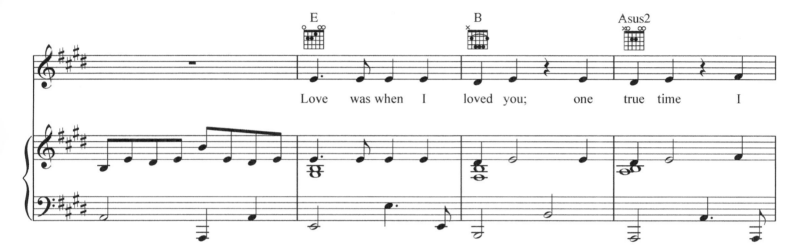

Love was when I loved you; one true time I

hold to. In my life we'll al - ways go on.

D.S. al Coda

CODA

on.

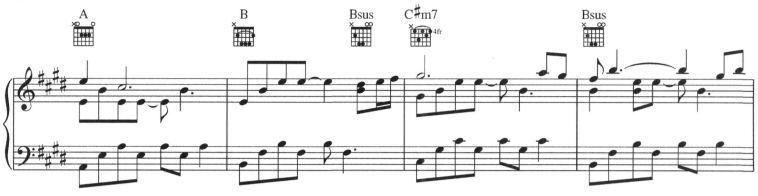

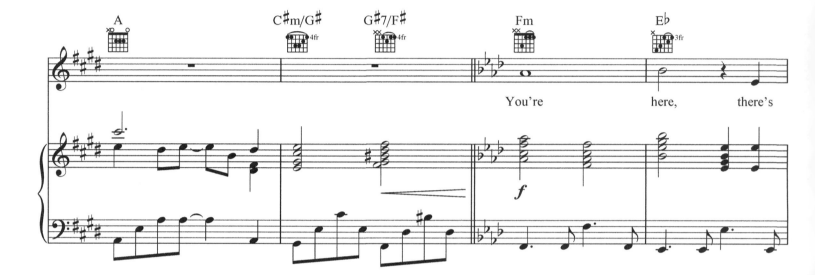

You're here, there's

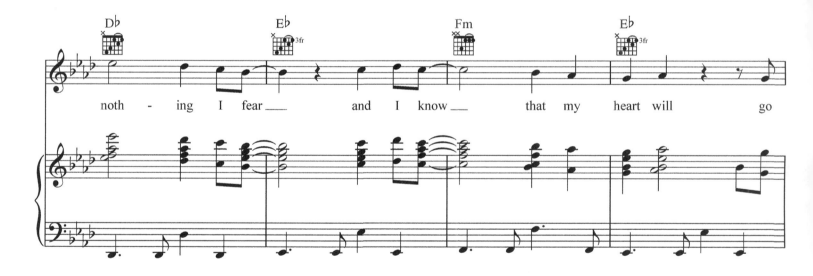

noth - ing I fear ___ and I know ___ that my heart will go

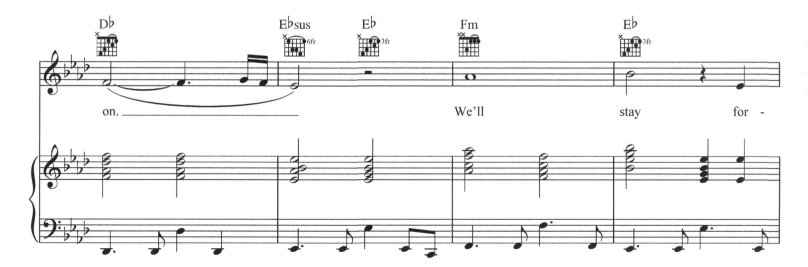

on. _____ We'll stay for -

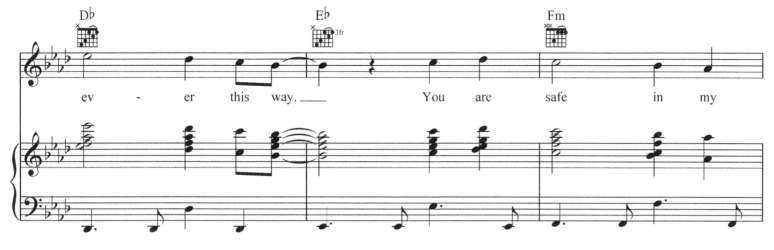

ev - er this way. ___ You are safe in my

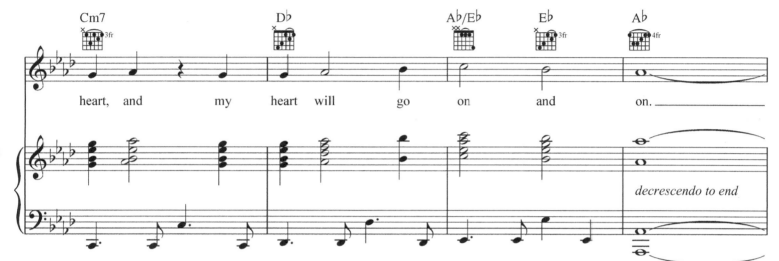

heart, and my heart will go on and on. ___

decrescendo to end

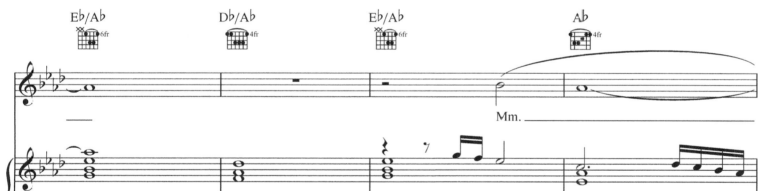

Mm. ___

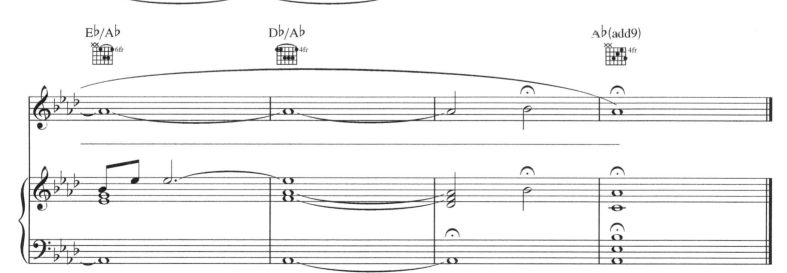

SAY SOMETHING

Words and Music by IAN AXEL,
CHAD VACCARINO and MIKE CAMPBELL

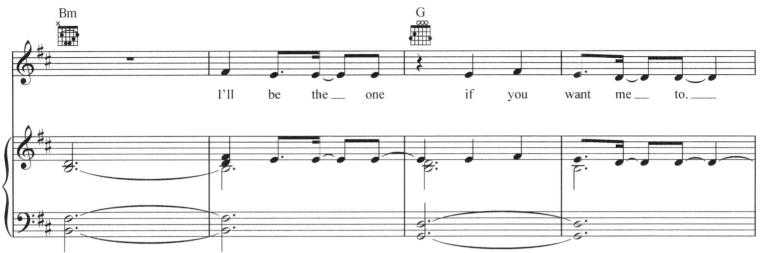

I'll be the __ one if you want me __ to. __

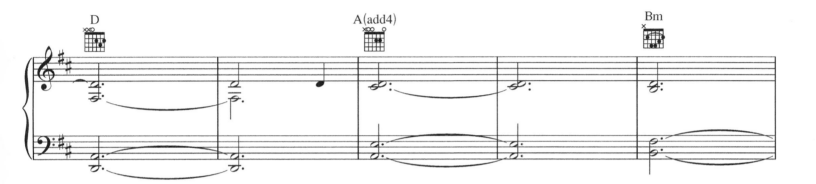

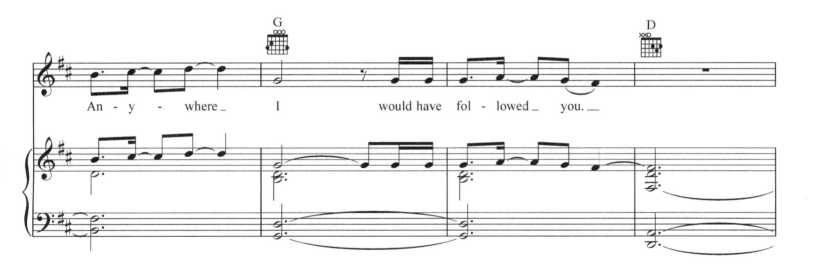

An - y - where __ I would have fol - lowed __ you. __

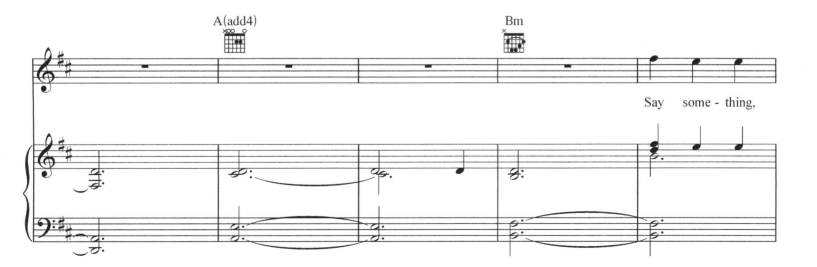

Say some - thing,

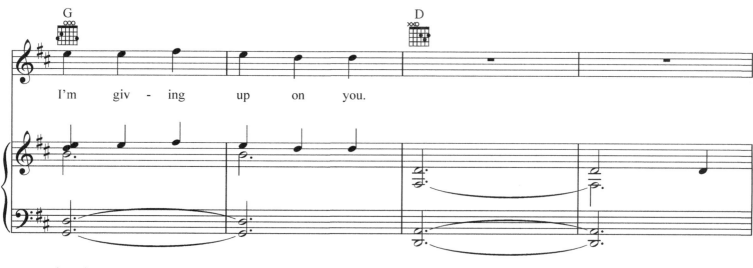

I'm giv - ing up on you.

And I

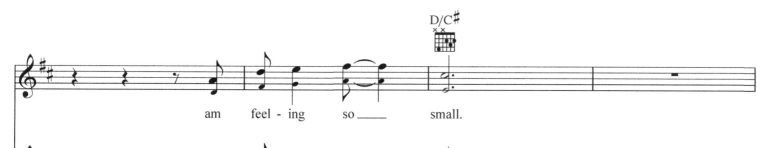

am feel - ing so ___ small.

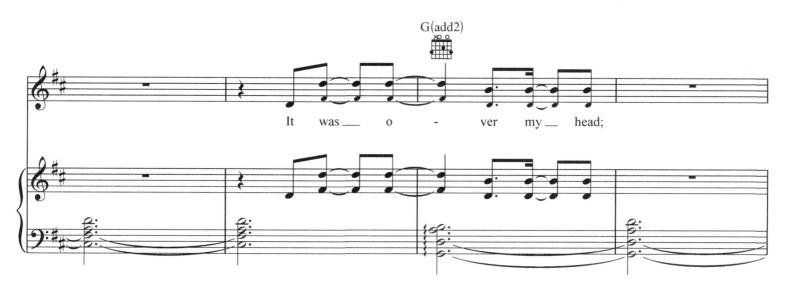

It was ___ o - ver my ___ head;

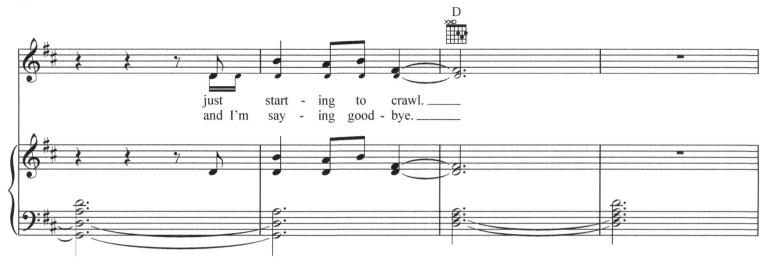

just start - ing to crawl. _____
and I'm say - ing good - bye. _____

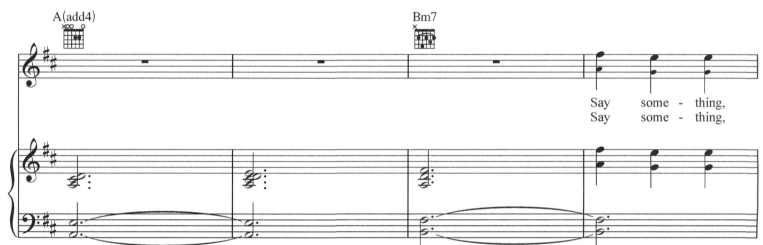

Say some - thing,
Say some - thing,

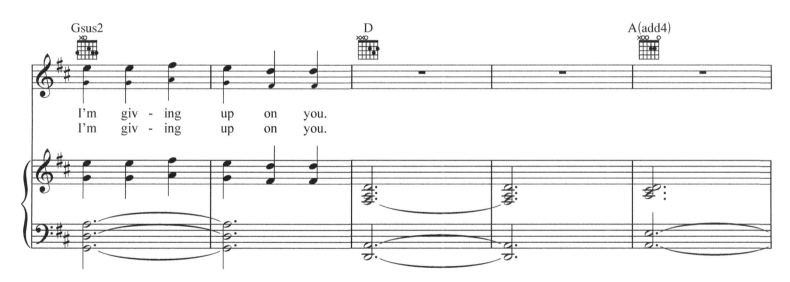

I'm giv - ing up on you.
I'm giv - ing up on you.

I'm sor - ry that I _____ could - n't _____ get _____
And I'm sor - ry that I _____ could - n't _____ get _____

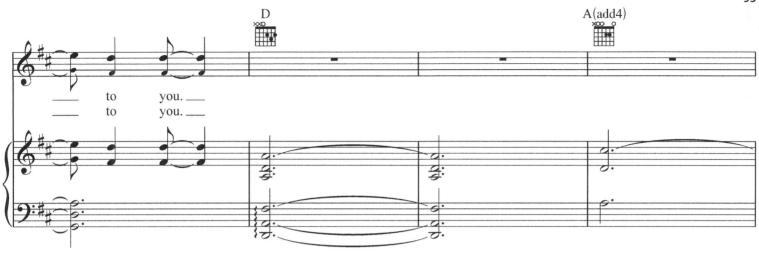

to you. ___
to you. ___

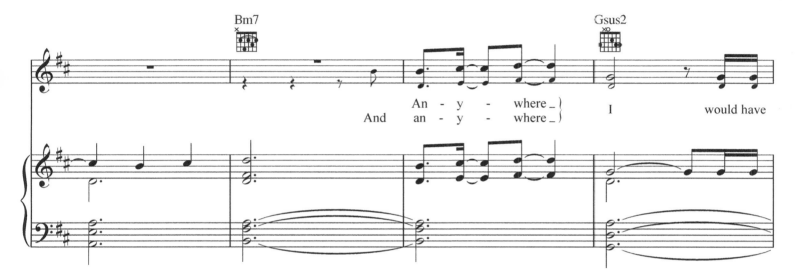

An - y - where ___ I would have
And an - y - where ___ I

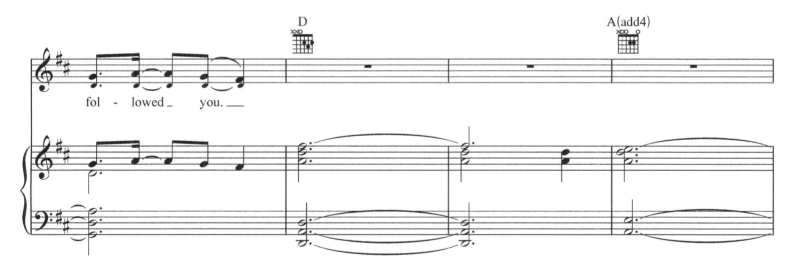

fol - lowed ___ you. ___

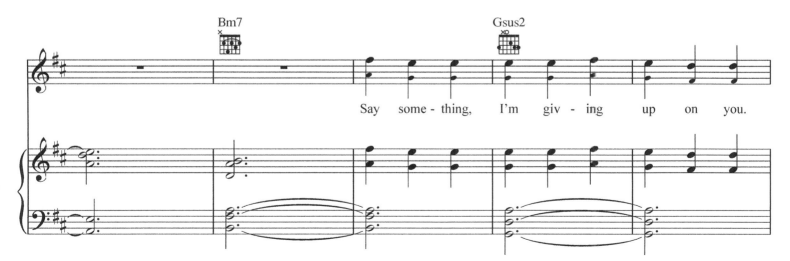

Say some - thing, I'm giv - ing up on you.

TEARS IN HEAVEN

Words and Music by ERIC CLAPTON
and WILL JENNINGS

Moderately relaxed tempo

Would you know my name _____
Would you hold my hand _____
Would you know my name _____

if I saw you in heav - en?
if I saw you in heav - en?
if I saw you in heav - en?

Would it be the same _____
Would you help me stand _____
Would you be the same _____

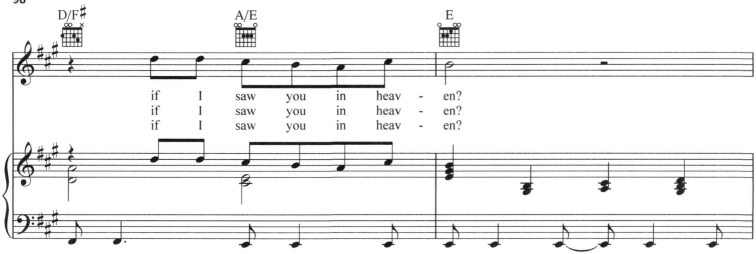

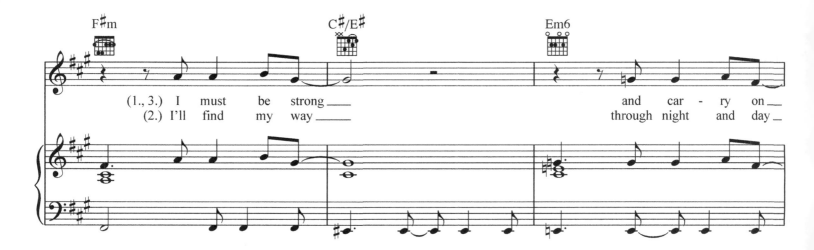

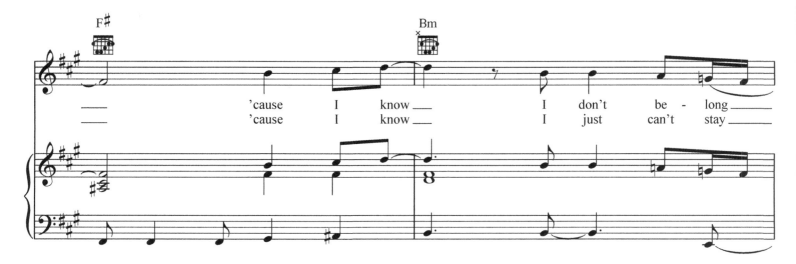

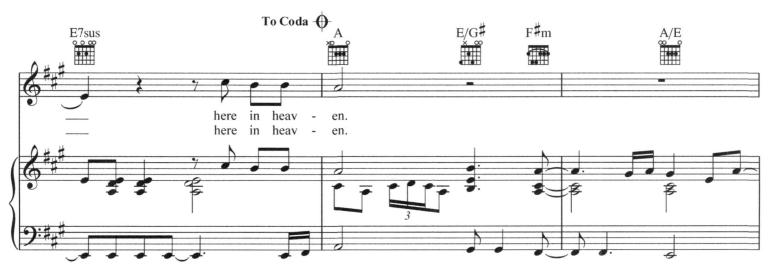

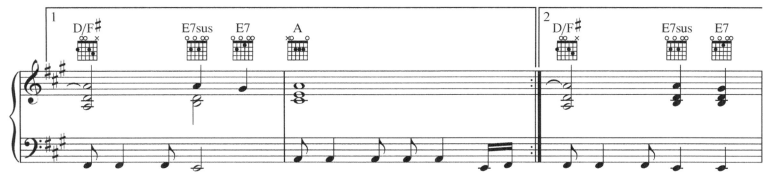

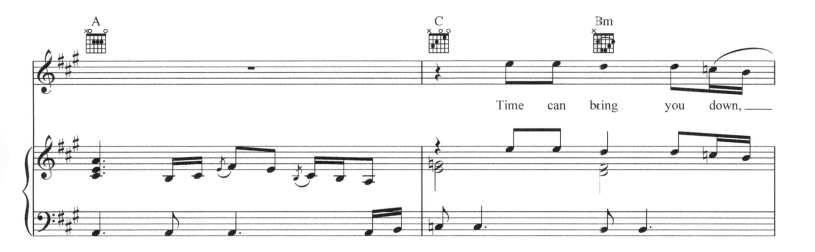

Time can bring you down, _____

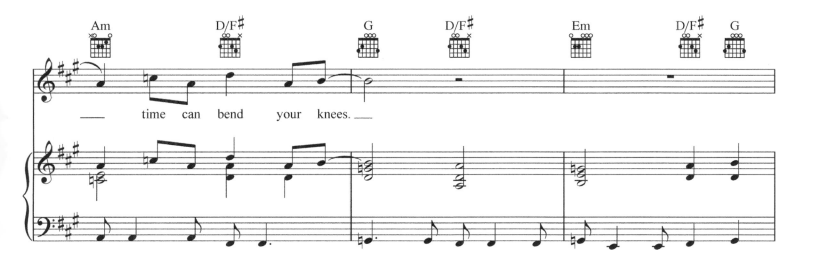

_____ time can bend your knees. _____

Time can break the heart, _____ have you beg - gin' please, _____ beg - gin' please. _

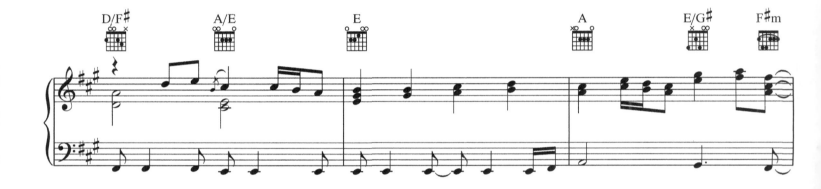

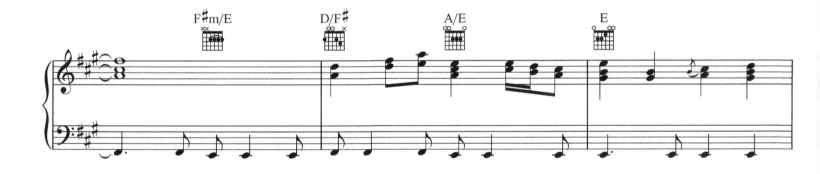

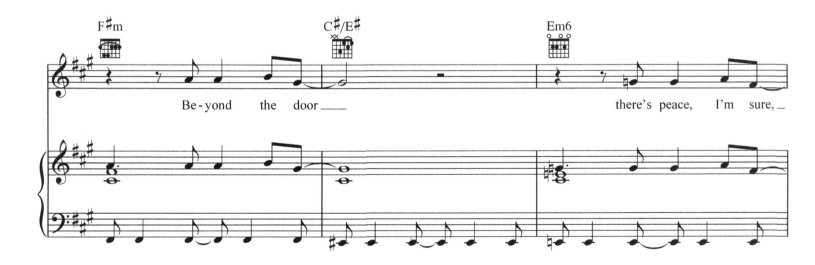

Be-yond the door ___ there's peace, I'm sure, ___

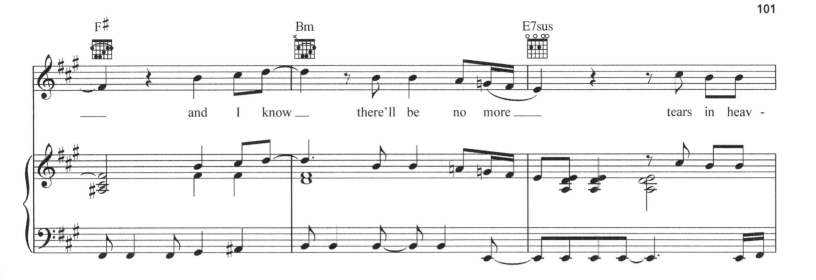

and I know ___ there'll be no more ___ tears in heav-

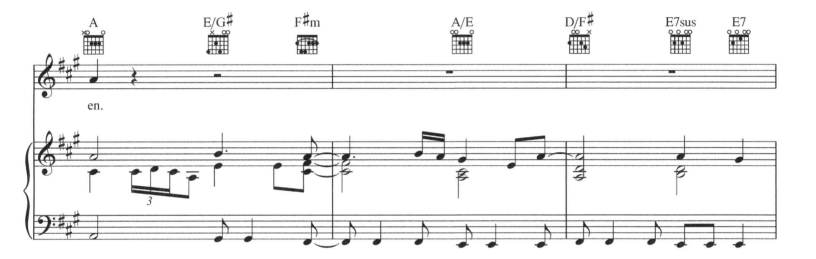

en.

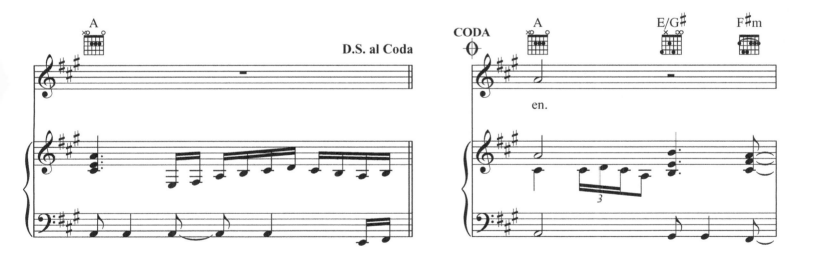

D.S. al Coda

CODA

en.

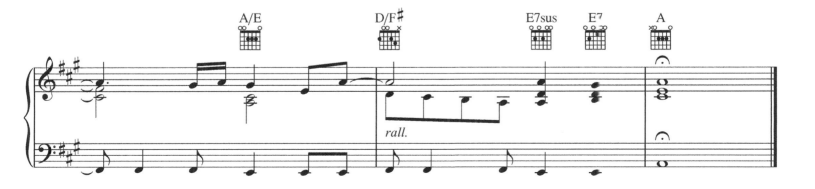

rall.

SOMEONE LIKE YOU

Words and Music by ADELE ADKINS
and DAN WILSON

Piano Ballad

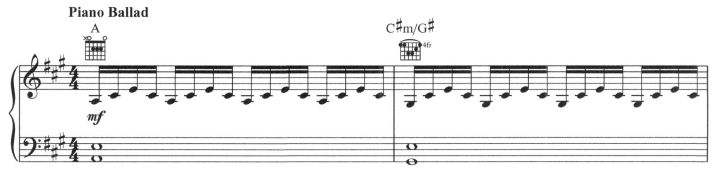

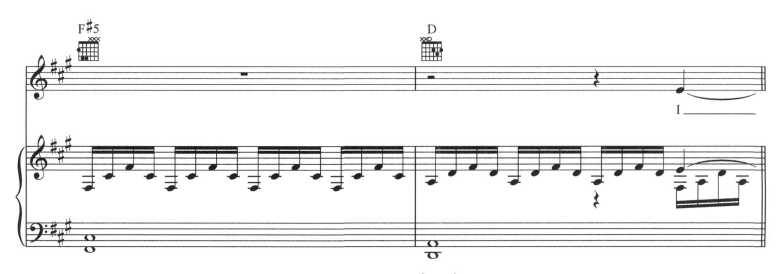

heard   that you're   set-tled down, _   that you

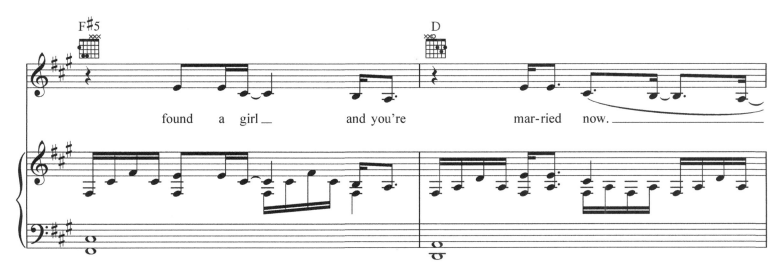

found   a girl _   and you're   mar-ried now. _____

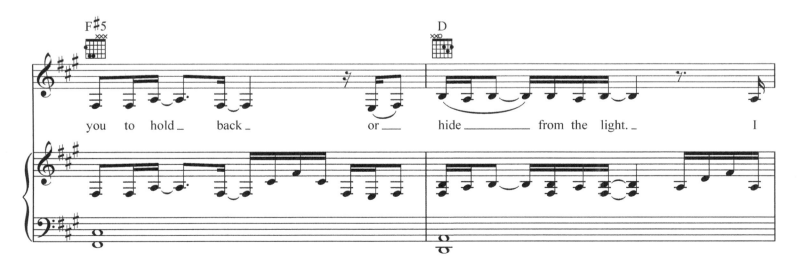

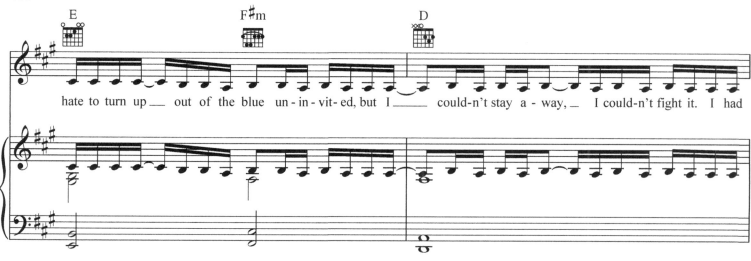

hate to turn up ___ out of the blue un-in-vit-ed, but I ___ could-n't stay a-way, ___ I could-n't fight it. I had

hoped you'd see my face and that you'd be re-mind-ed that, for me, ___ it is-n't o - ver. ___

___ Nev - er mind, ___ I'll ___ find ___ some-one like ___

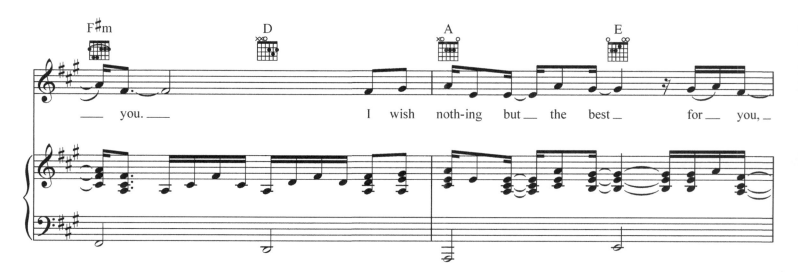

___ you. ___ I wish noth-ing but ___ the best ___ for ___ you, ___

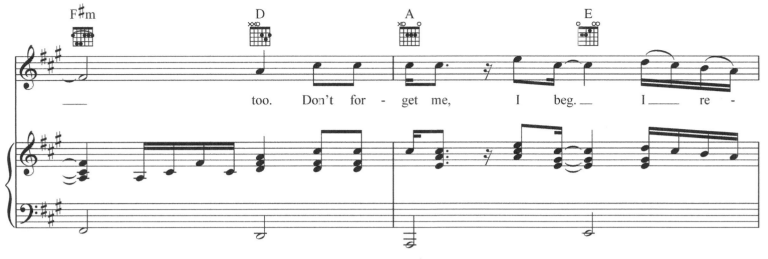

too. Don't for-get me, I beg. __ I __ re-

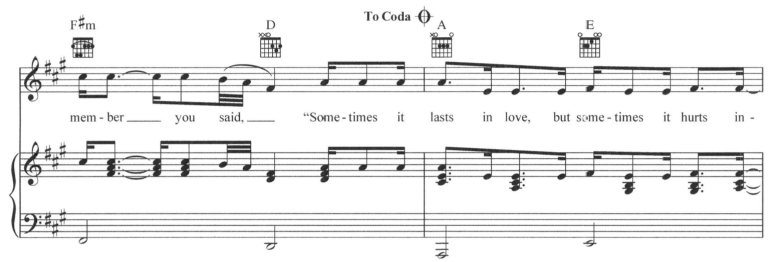

mem-ber __ you said, __ "Some-times it lasts in love, but some-times it hurts in-

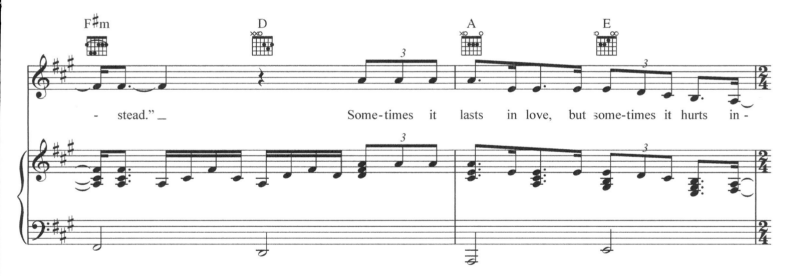

-stead." __ Some-times it lasts in love, but some-times it hurts in-

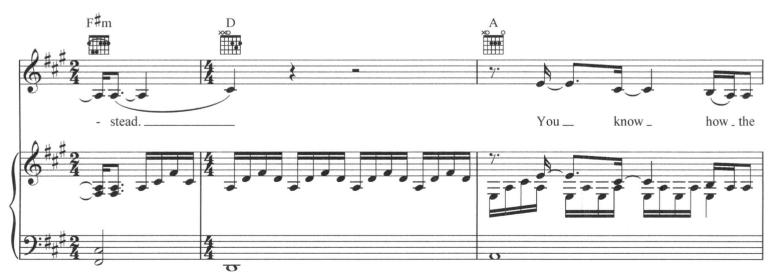

-stead. _____ You __ know __ how __ the

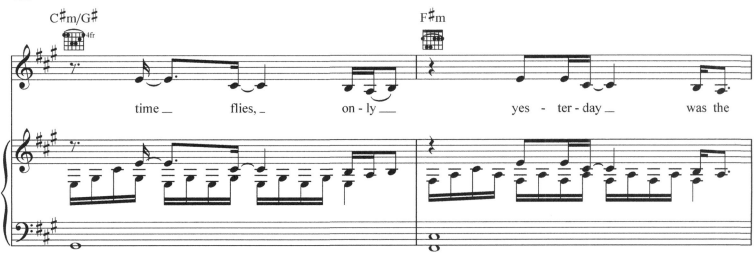

time ___ flies, ___ on - ly ___ yes - ter - day ___ was the

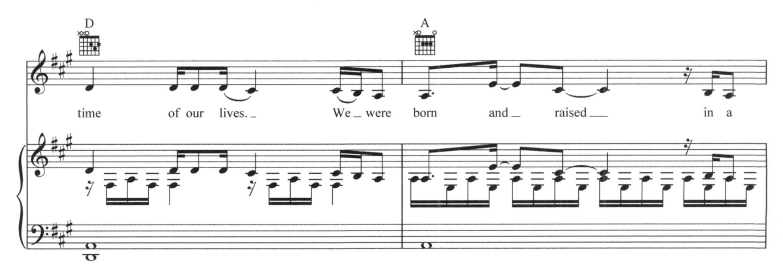

time of our lives. ___ We ___ were born and ___ raised ___ in a

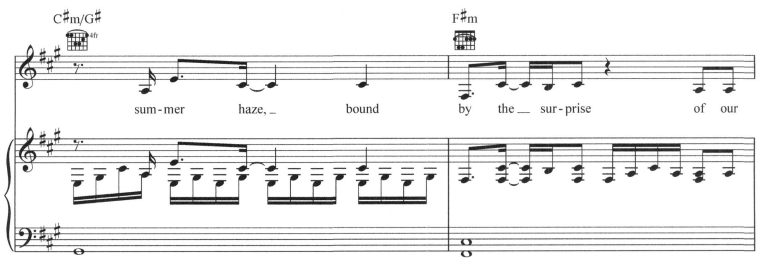

sum - mer haze, ___ bound by the ___ sur - prise of our

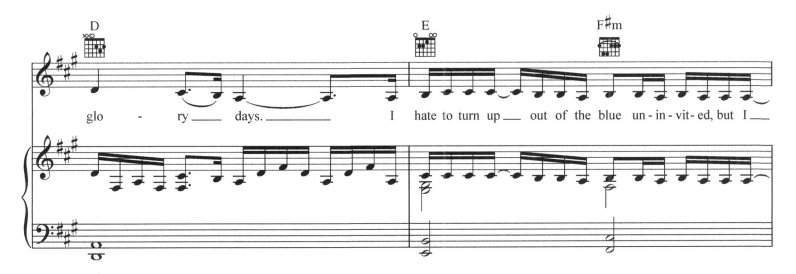

glo - ry ___ days. ___ I hate to turn up ___ out of the blue un - in - vit - ed, but I ___

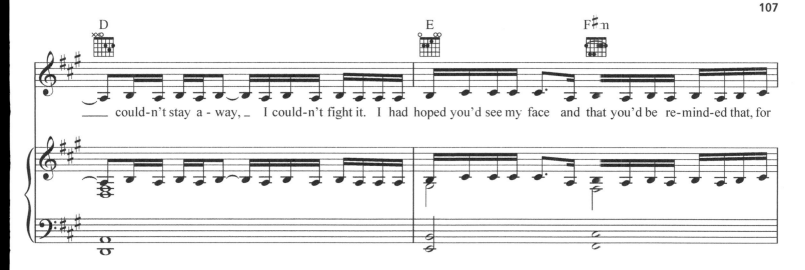

could-n't stay a - way, _ I could-n't fight it. I had hoped you'd see my face and that you'd be re-mind-ed that, for

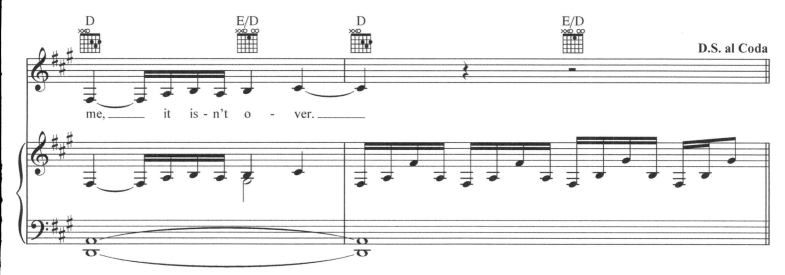

D.S. al Coda

me, _ it is-n't o - ver. _

CODA

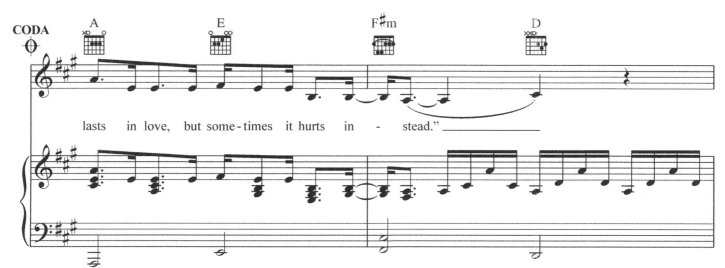

lasts in love, but some-times it hurts in - stead." _

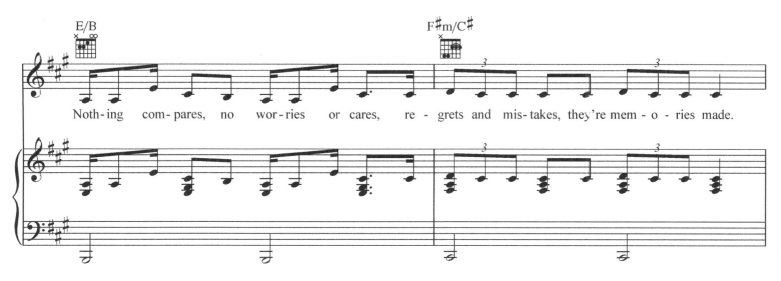

Noth-ing com-pares, no wor-ries or cares, re - grets and mis-takes, they're mem - o - ries made.

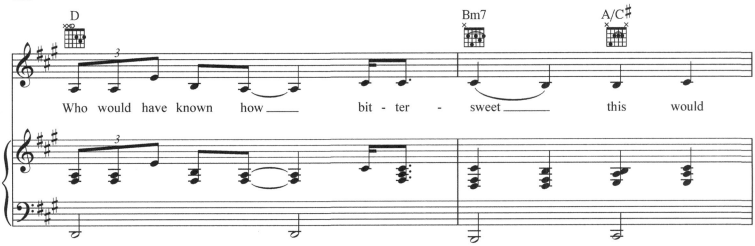

Who would have known how ____ bit - ter - sweet ____ this would

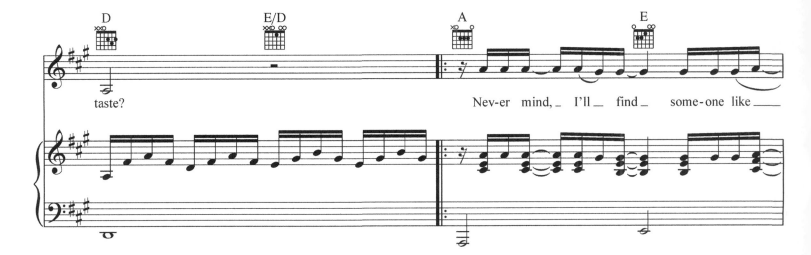

taste? Nev-er mind, _ I'll _ find _ some-one like ____

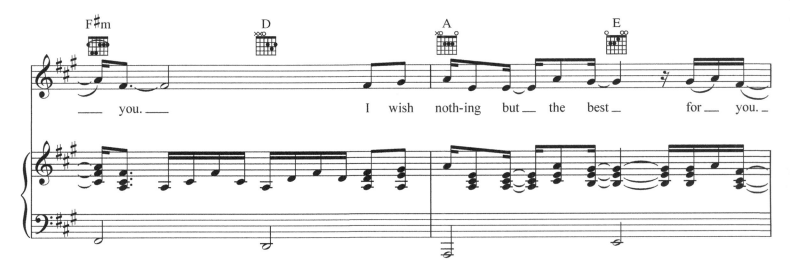

___ you. ___ I wish noth-ing but _ the best _ for _ you. _

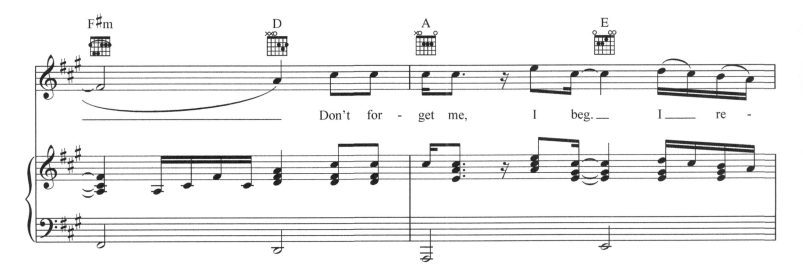

____ Don't for - get me, I beg. _ I re -

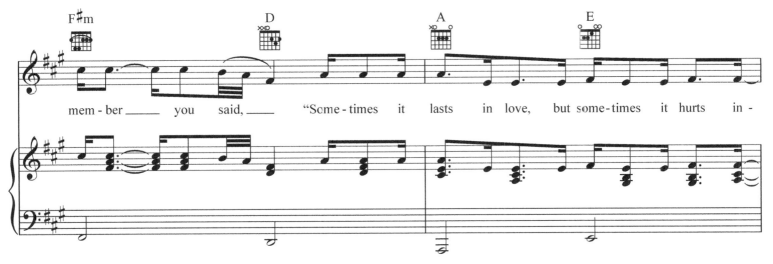

mem - ber _____ you said, _____ "Some-times it lasts in love, but some-times it hurts in -

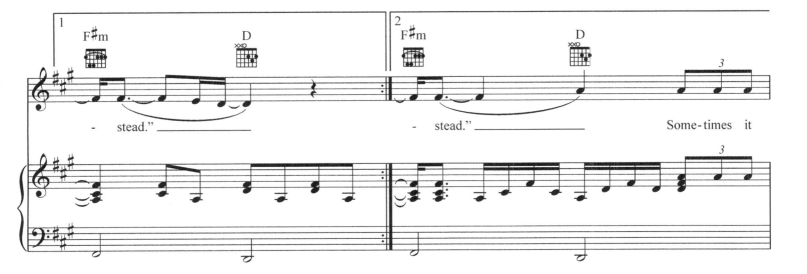

- stead." _____ - stead." _____ Some-times it

lasts in love, but some-times it hurts in - stead. _____

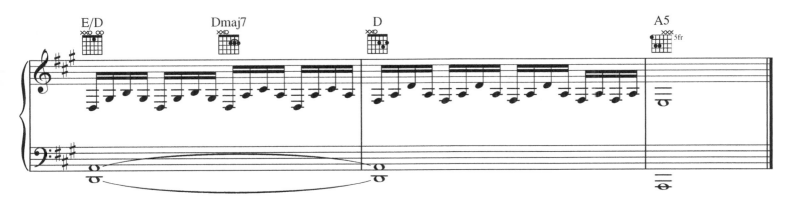

STAY WITH ME

Words and Music by SAM SMITH,
JAMES NAPIER, WILLIAM EDWARD PHILLIPS,
TOM PETTY and JEFF LYNNE

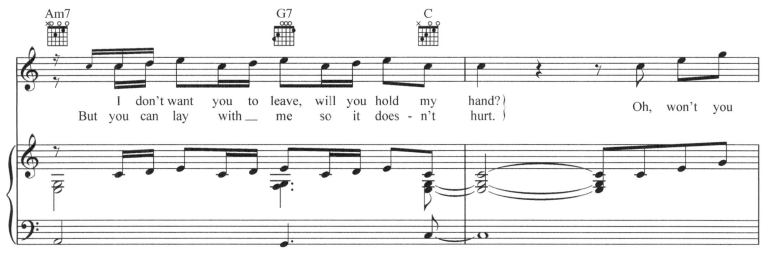

I don't want you to leave, will you hold my hand?
But you can lay with me so it does-n't hurt.
Oh, won't you

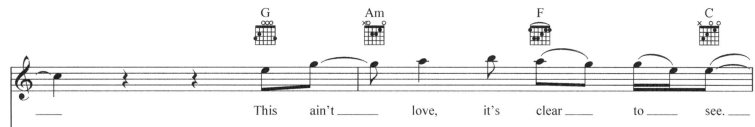

stay with me? 'Cause you're all I need.

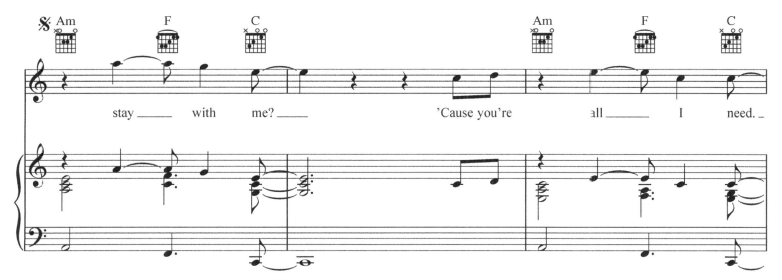

This ain't love, it's clear to see.

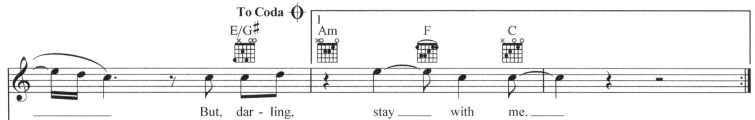

But, dar-ling, stay with me.

'Cause you're all ___ I need. ___ This ain't ___

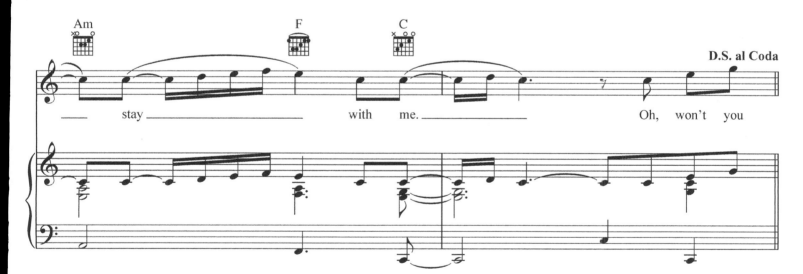

___ love, it's clear ___ to ___ see. But, dar - ling, ___

D.S. al Coda

___ stay ___ with me. ___ Oh, won't you

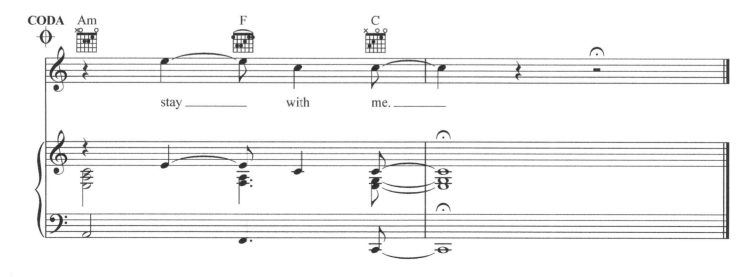

CODA

stay ___ with me. ___

TIME IN A BOTTLE

Words and Music by
JIM CROCE

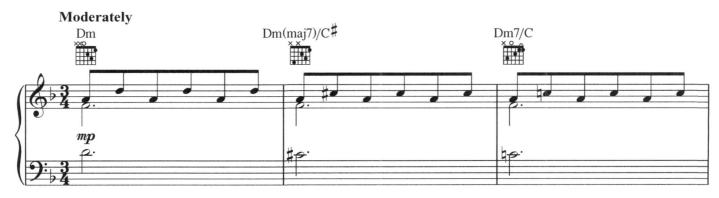

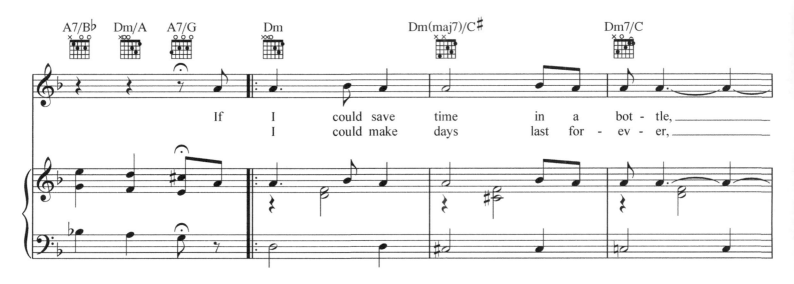

If I could save time in a bot - tle, _____
I could make days last for - ev - er, _____

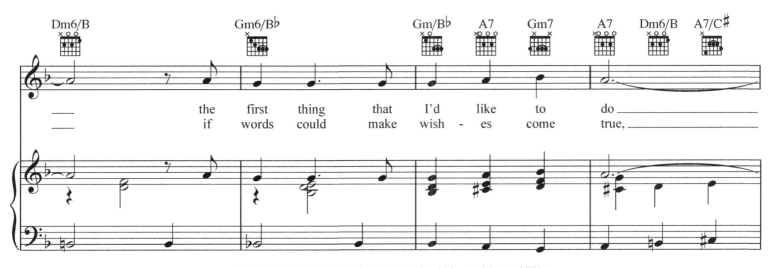

___ the first thing that I'd like to do _____
___ if words could that make wish - es come true, _____

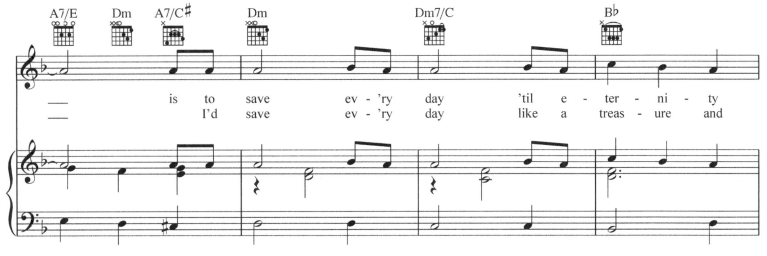

is to save ev - 'ry day 'til e - ter - ni - ty
I'd save ev - 'ry day like a treas - ure and

pass - es a - way just to spend them with you.
then a - gain I would spend them with you.

If But there nev - er seems to

be e - nough time to do the things you want to do once you

find them. _____ I've

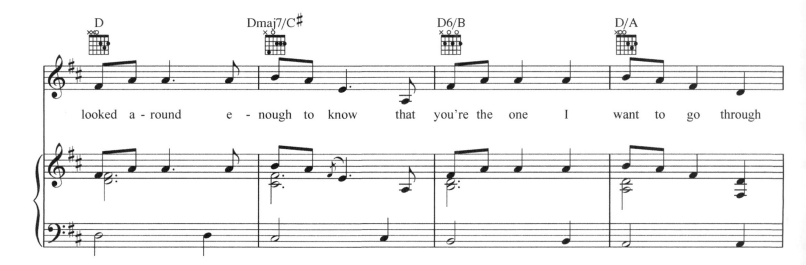

looked a - round e - nough to know that you're the one I want to go through

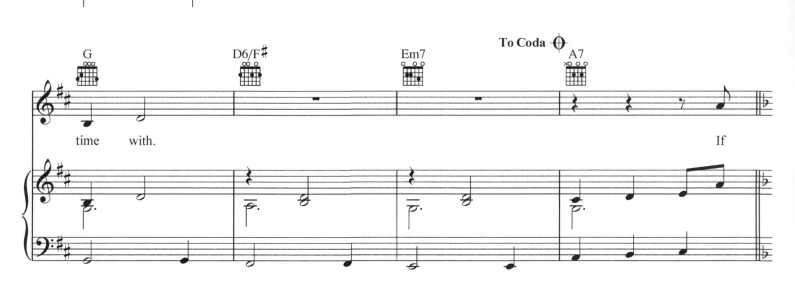

time with. If

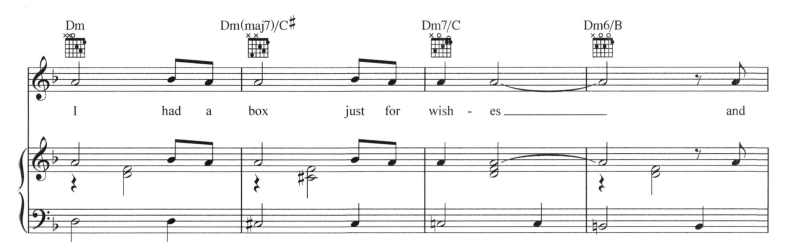

I had a box just for wish - es _____ and

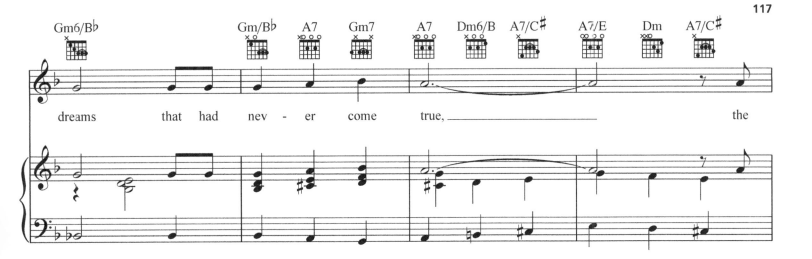

dreams that had nev - er come true, _____ the

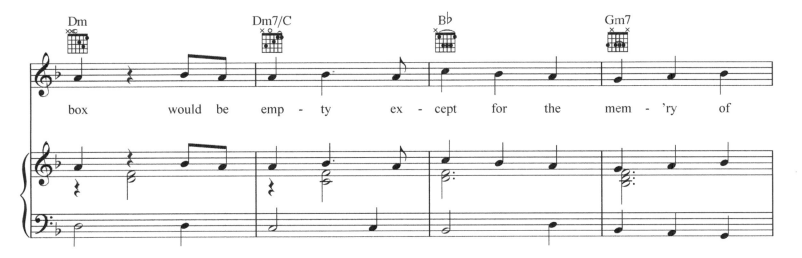

box would be emp - ty ex - cept for the mem - 'ry of

how they were an - swered by you. _____ But there

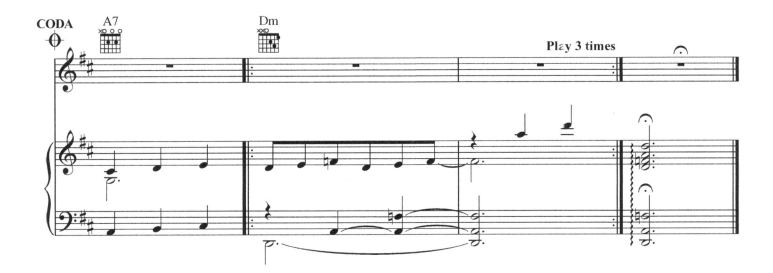

TRUE COLORS

Words and Music by BILLY STEINBERG
and TOM KELLY

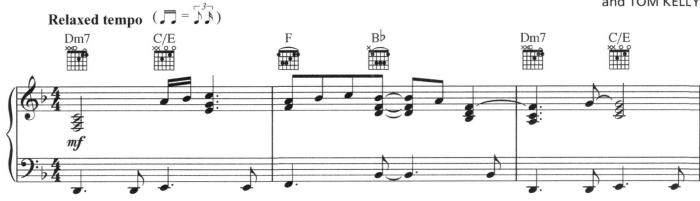

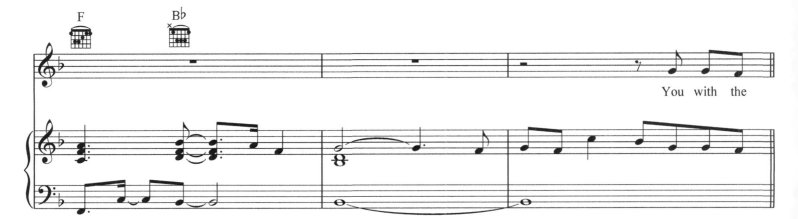

You with the

sad   eyes,   don't be dis-cour-aged. Oh, I re-al-ize   it's
smile then,   don't be un-hap-py. Can't re-mem-ber when   I

hard   to take cour-age.   In a world   full of peo-ple
last saw you laugh-ing.   If this world makes you   cra-zy   and you're

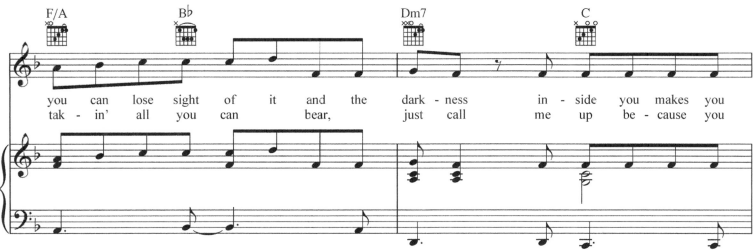

you can lose sight of it and the dark-ness in-side you makes you
tak-in' all you can bear, just call me up be-cause you

feel so small. But I } see your true col - ors shin -
know I'll be there. And I'll }

-in' through. I see your true col - ors and that's why I love __ you. So,

don't be a-fraid __ to let them show. __ Your true col - ors,

true col - ors are beau-ti-ful, ooh, __ like a rain - bow.

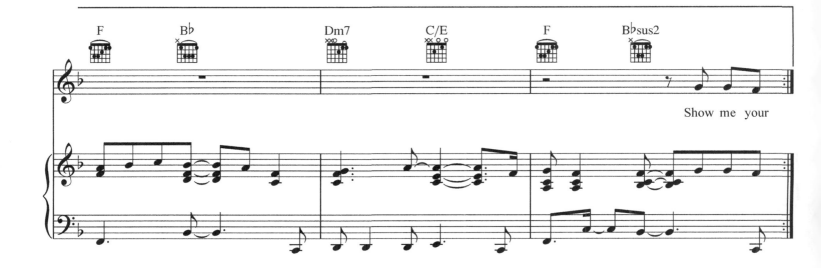

Show me your

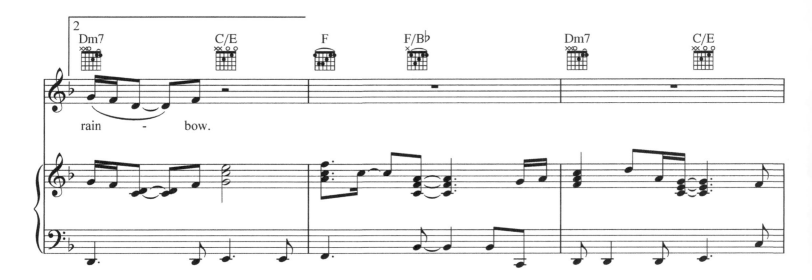

rain - bow.

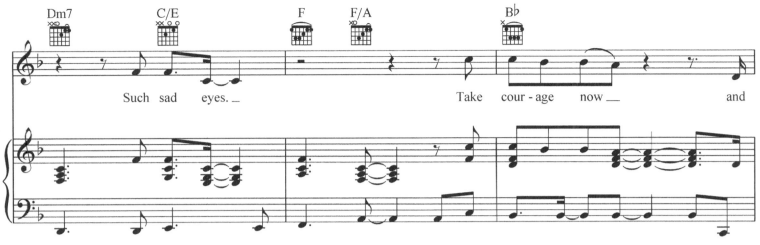

-in' through. I see your true col - ors and

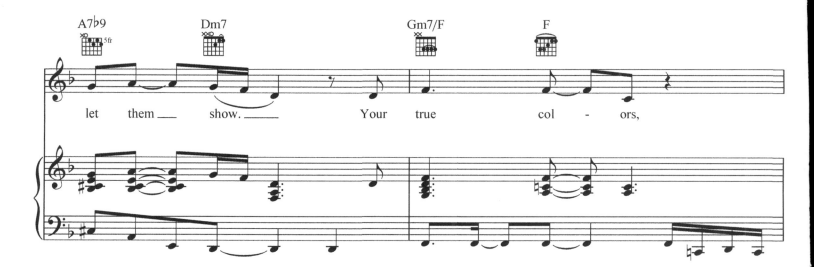

that's why I love ____ you. So, don't be a - fraid, ____ just

let them ____ show. ____ Your true col - ors,

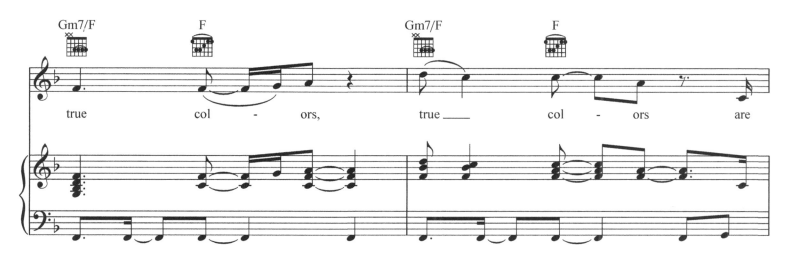

true col - ors, true ____ col - ors are

beau - ti - ful,   beau - ti - ful like a rain - bow.

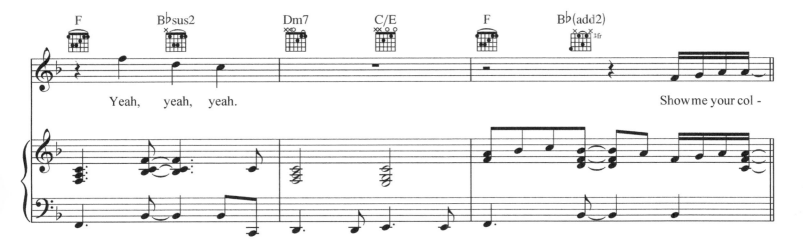

Yeah,   yeah,   yeah.   Show me your col -

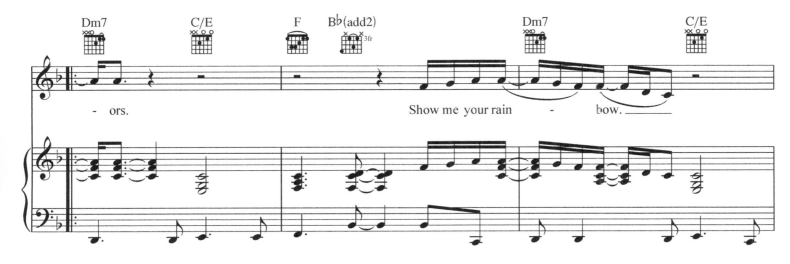

- ors.   Show me your rain - bow. _____

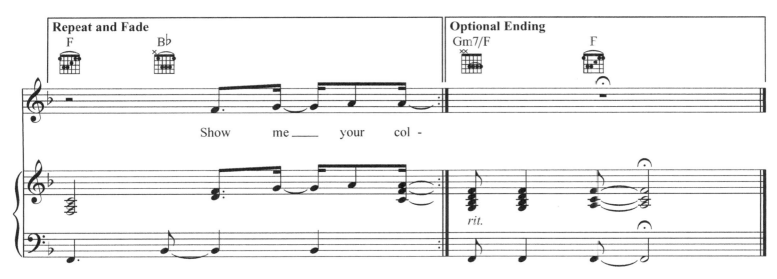

Repeat and Fade

Show me _____ your col -

Optional Ending

rit.

UP WHERE WE BELONG

from the Paramount Picture AN OFFICER AND A GENTLEMAN

Words by WILL JENNINGS
Music by BUFFY SAINTE-MARIE and JACK NITZSCHE

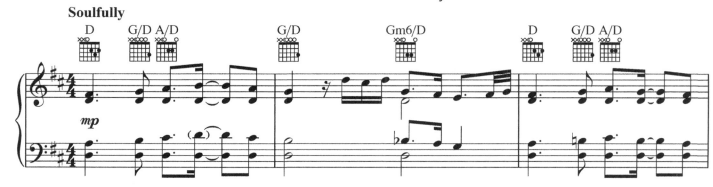

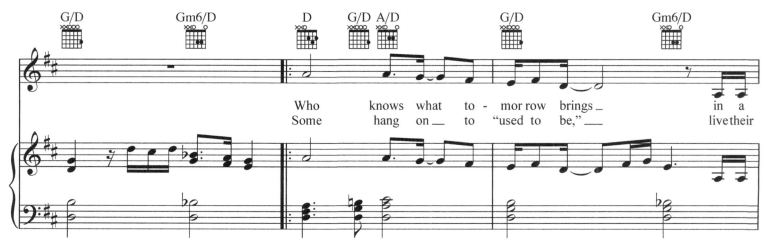

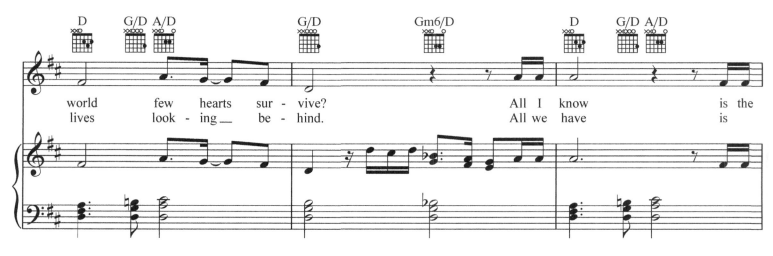

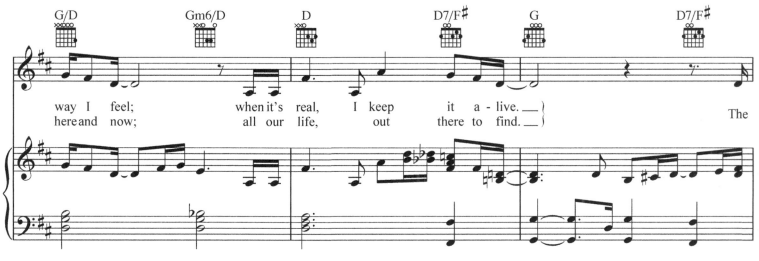

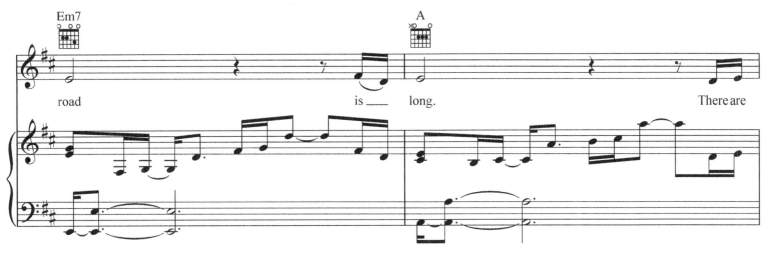

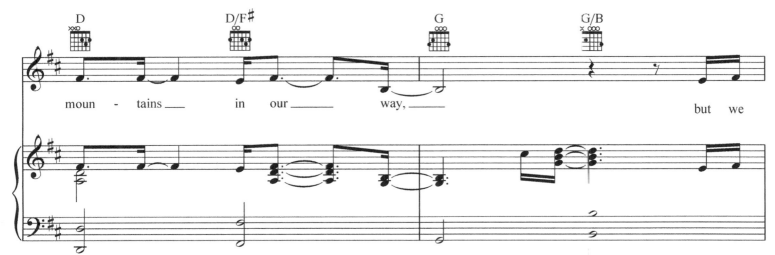

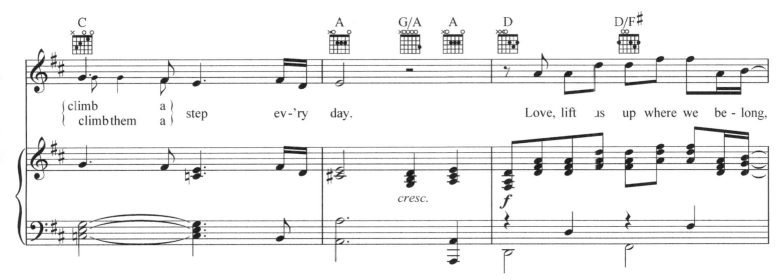

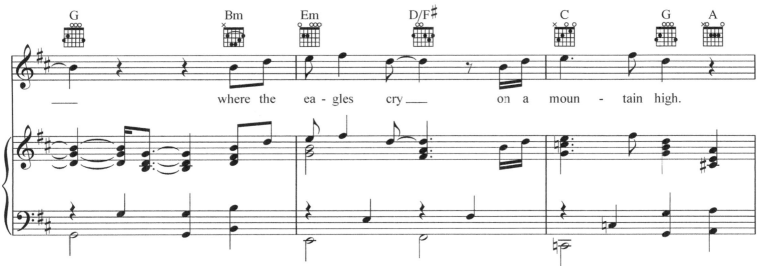

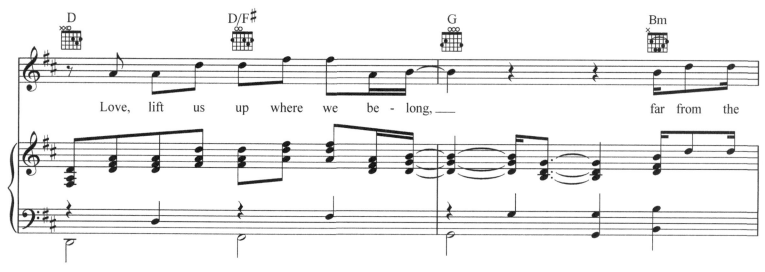

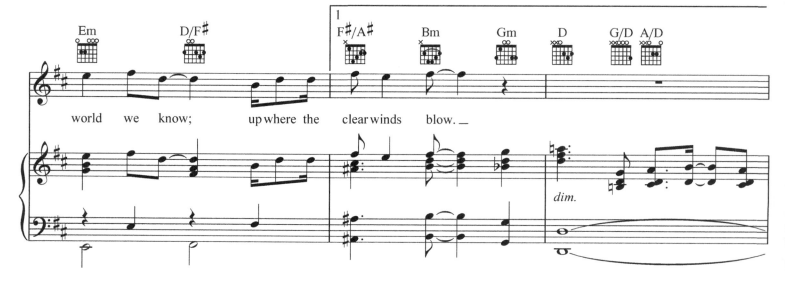

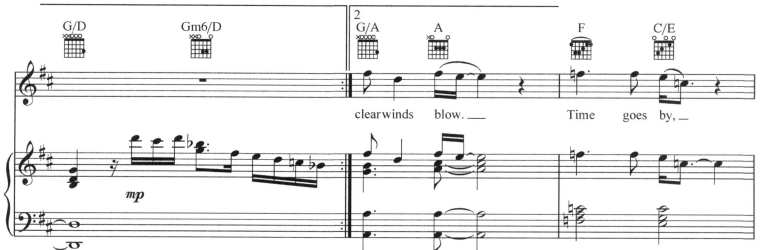

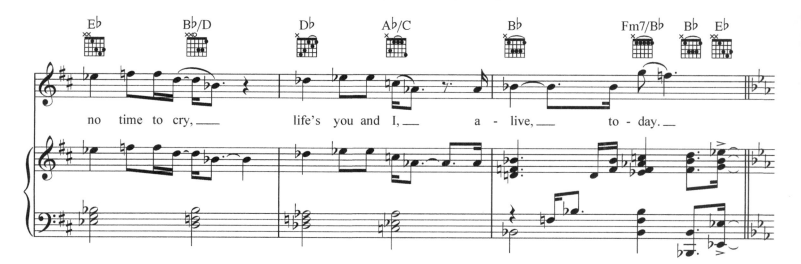

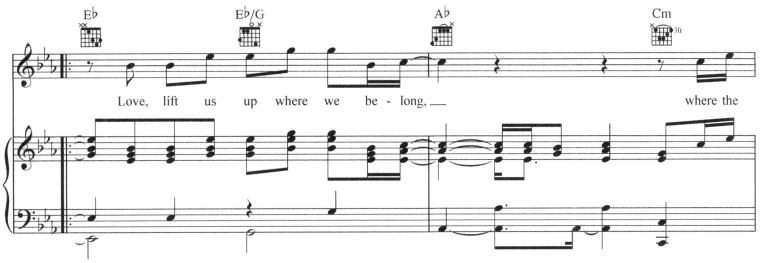

Love, lift us up where we be - long, ___ where the

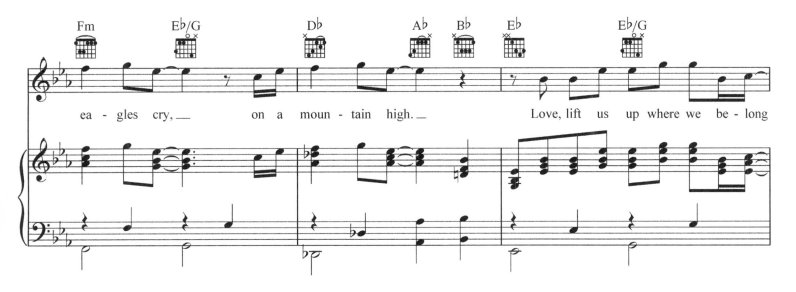

ea - gles cry, ___ on a moun - tain high. ___ Love, lift us up where we be - long

Repeat and Fade

___ far from the world we know; ___ where the clear winds blow. ___

Optional Ending

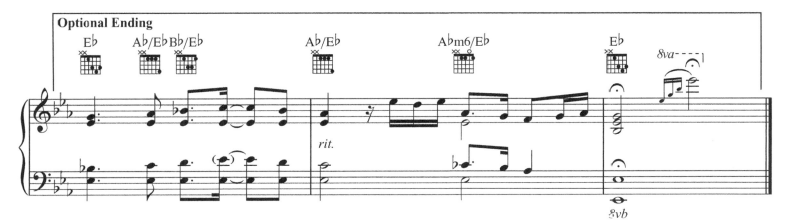

rit.

YOU RAISE ME UP

Words and Music by BRENDAN GRAHAM
and ROLF LOVLAND

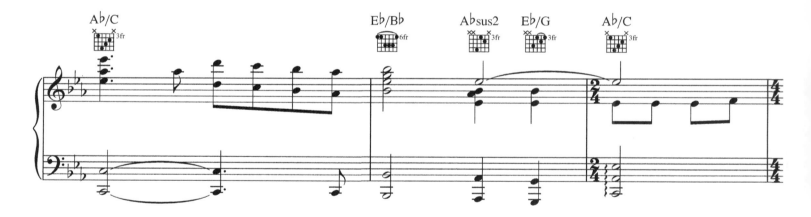

When I am down ___ and oh, my soul's so wea-ry, when trou-bles

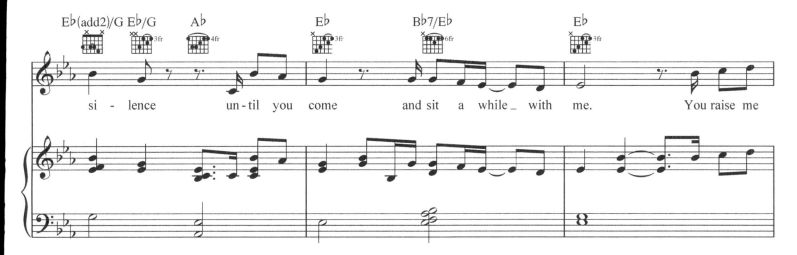

come and my heart ___ bur-dened be, then I am still ___ and wait here in the

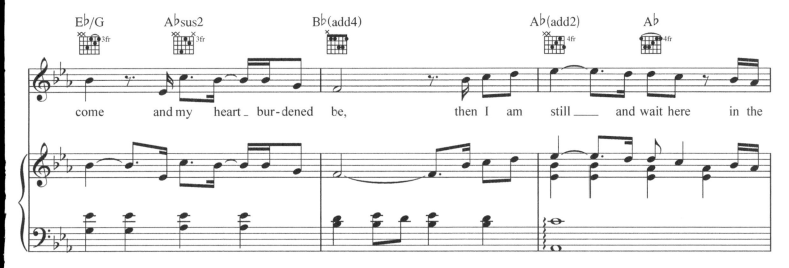

si - lence un - til you come and sit a while ___ with me. You raise me

up so I can stand on moun - tains. You raise me up to walk on storm - y

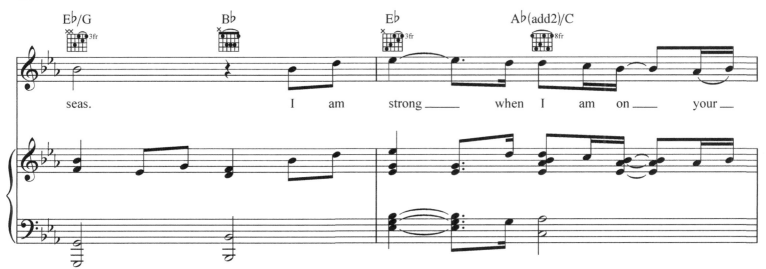

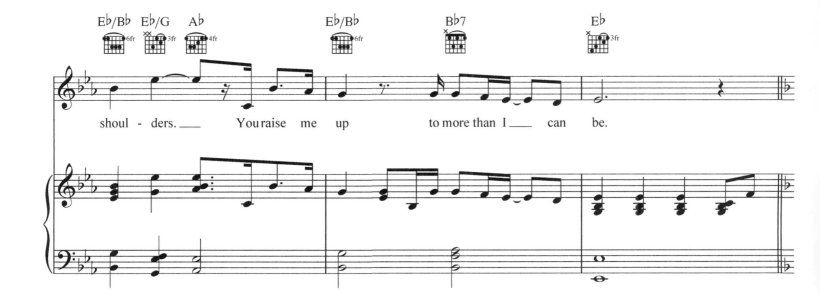

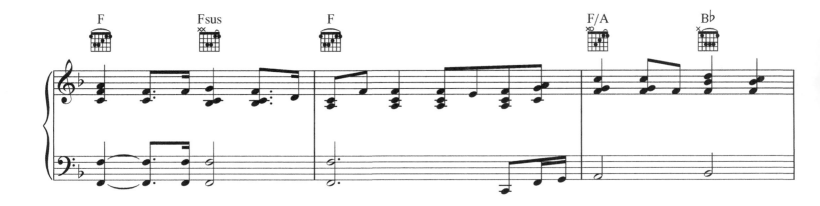

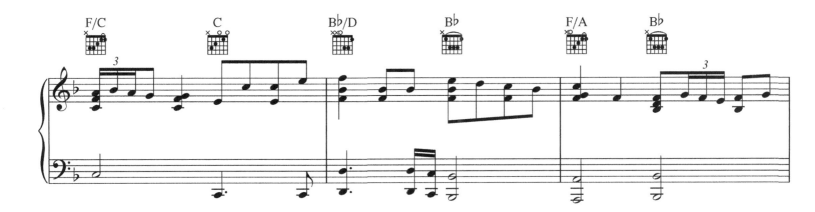

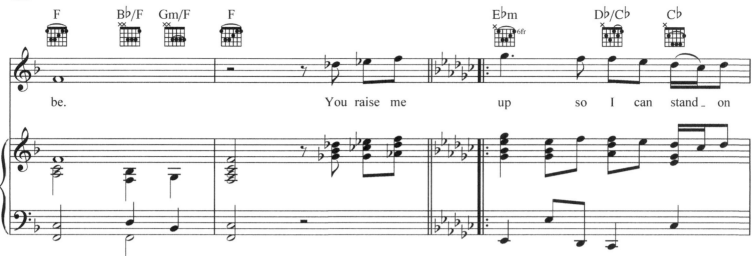

be. You raise me up so I can stand on

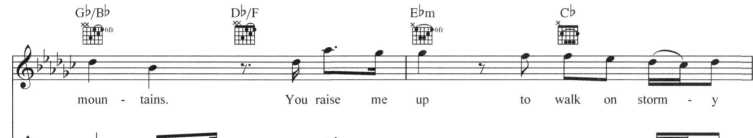

moun - tains. You raise me up to walk on storm - y

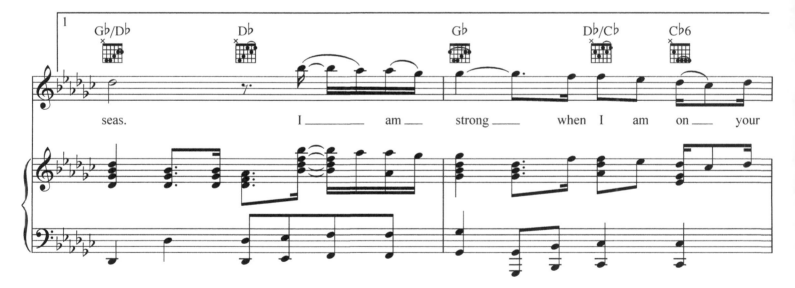

seas. I __ am __ strong __ when I am on __ your

shoul - ders. You raise me up to more than I __ can

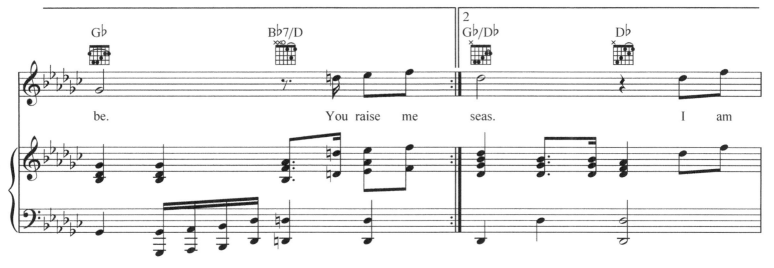

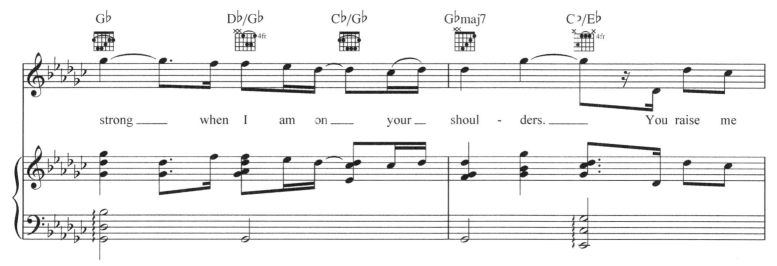

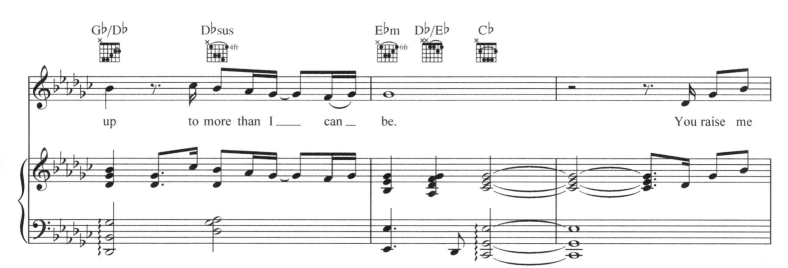

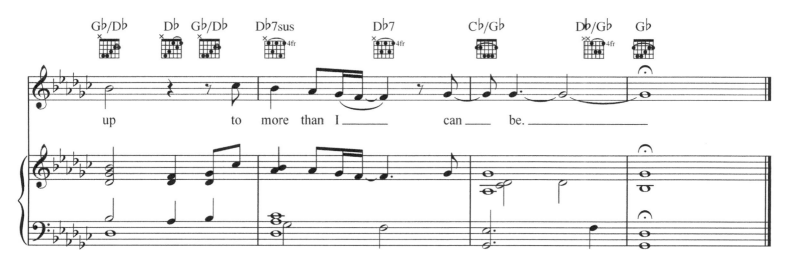

YOU'VE GOT A FRIEND

Words and Music by
CAROLE KING

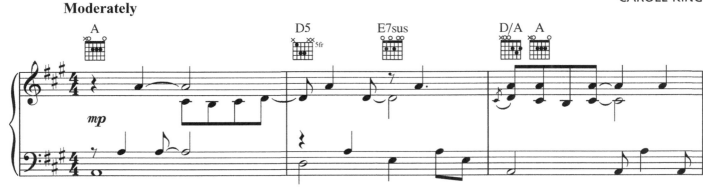

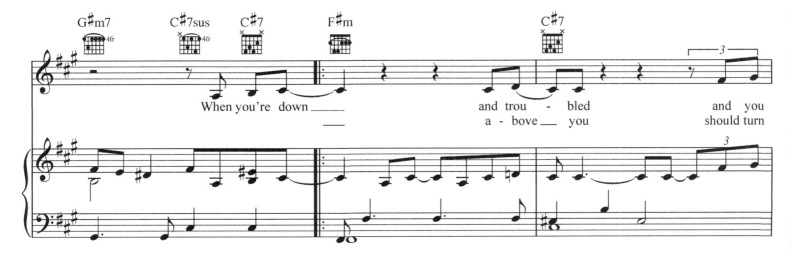

When you're down _____ and trou - bled and you
a - bove _____ you should turn

need a help - ing hand _____ and noth - ing, whoa,
dark and full of clouds _____ and that old north

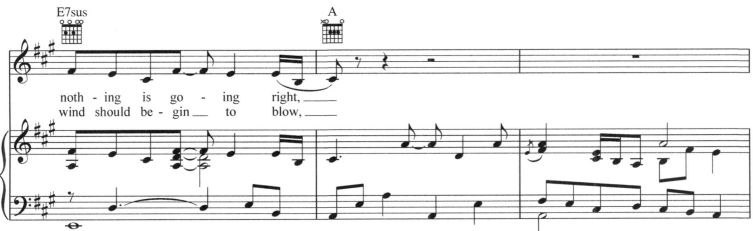

noth - ing is go - ing right, _____
wind should be - gin _____ to blow, _____

close your eyes___ and think of me and soon I will___ be there___
keep your head___ to-geth - er and call my name_____ out

___ loud,_____ now;___ to bright-en up soon I'll be knock - ing up-on___ your e - ven your dark - est night. door.___

You just call_____ out my name,_

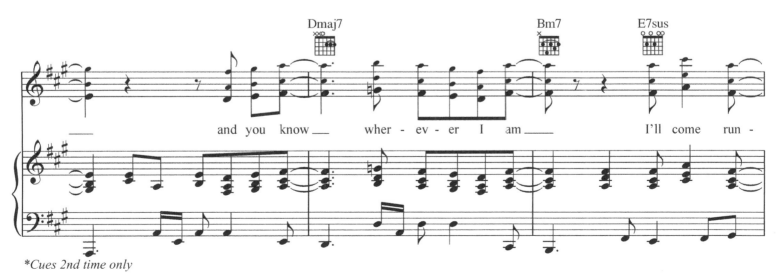

and you know___ wher - ev - er I am_____ I'll come run -

*Cues 2nd time only

-ning,
{ oh, __ yeah, ba — by, }
{ oh, __ yes, I ____ will, }
to see you a - gain. ___

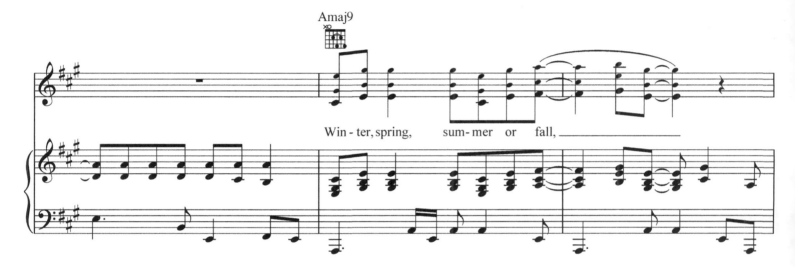

Win - ter, spring, sum- mer or fall, _____

all you've got to do __ is _____ call ___ and I'll be there, ___ yeah _ yeah, yeah; _

__ you've got a friend. ___

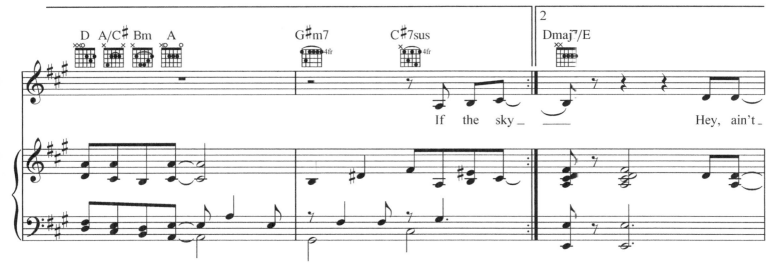

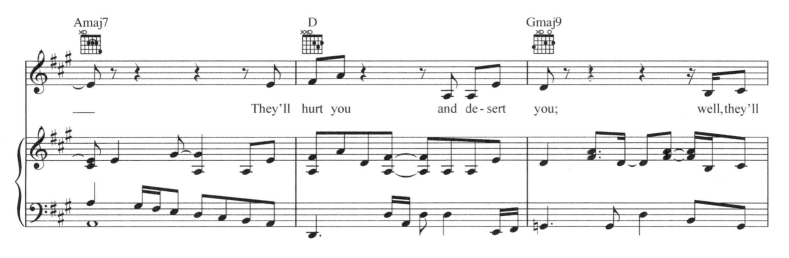

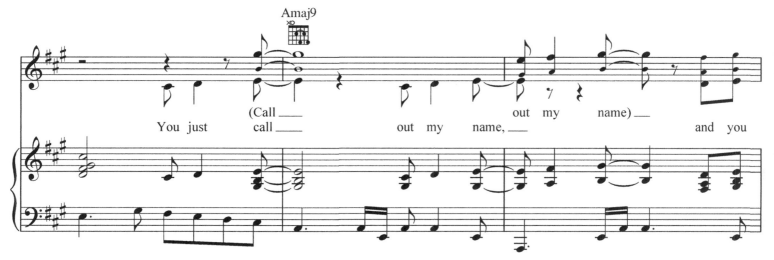

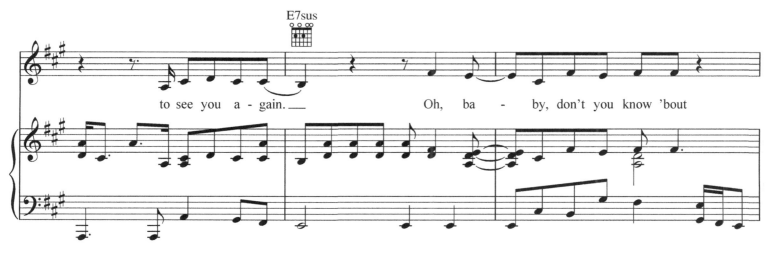

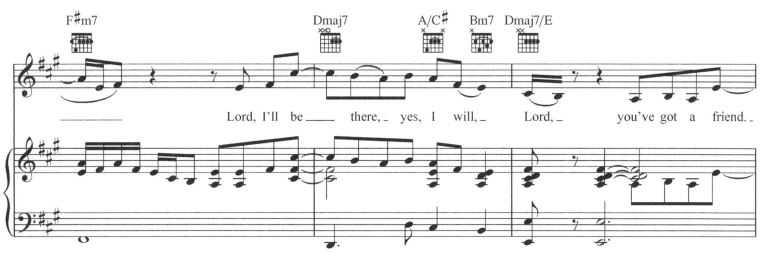

Lord, I'll be ___ there, _ yes, I will, _ Lord, _ you've got a friend. _

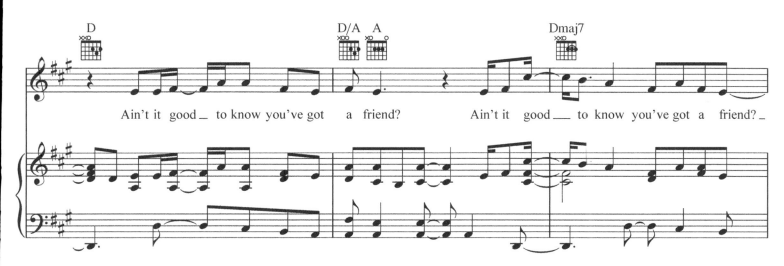

You've _ got a friend, _ yeah.

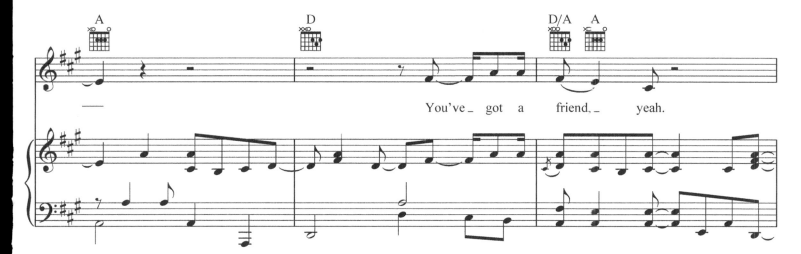

Ain't it good _ to know you've got a friend? Ain't it good ___ to know you've got a friend? _

Oh, yeah, ___ yeah, you've got a friend. ___

THINKING OUT LOUD

Words and Music by ED SHEERAN
and AMY WADGE

will be lov-ing you till ___ we're se - ven - ty. ___ And ba - by, my
soul could nev - er grow old, ___ it's ev - er - green. _ And ba - by, your

heart could still feel as hard __ at twen - ty - three. _____
smile's for - ev - er in my mind _ and mem - o - ry. _____

And I'm think-ing 'bout how ___ peo-ple fall in love in mys - te - ri-ous ways, __
And I'm think-ing 'bout how ___ peo-ple fall in love in mys - te - ri-ous ways, __ and

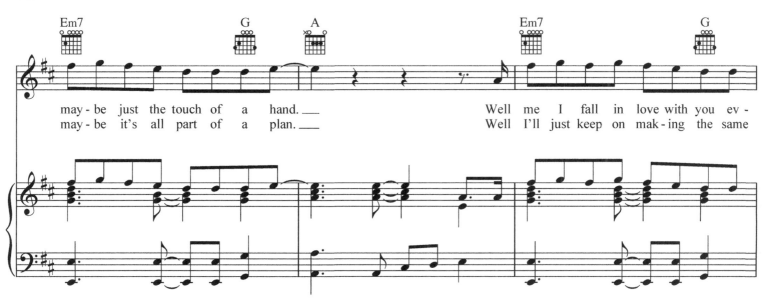

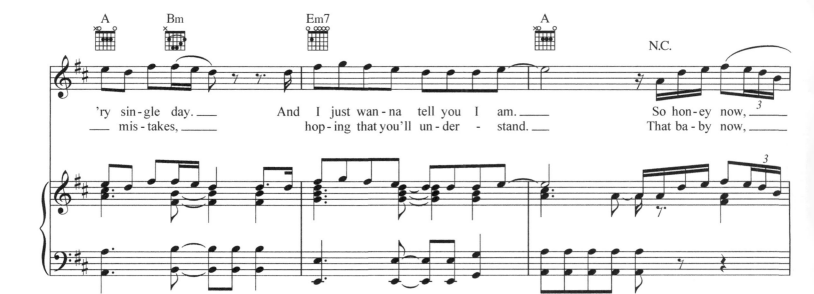

Kiss me un-der the light of a thou-sand stars. ___ Place your head on my beat-ing heart. ___

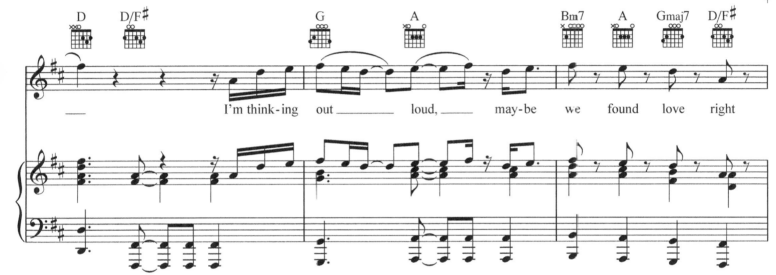

I'm think-ing out ___ loud, ___ may-be we found love right

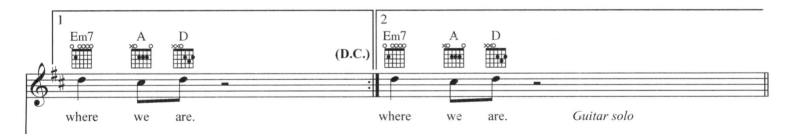

where we are. where we are. *Guitar solo*

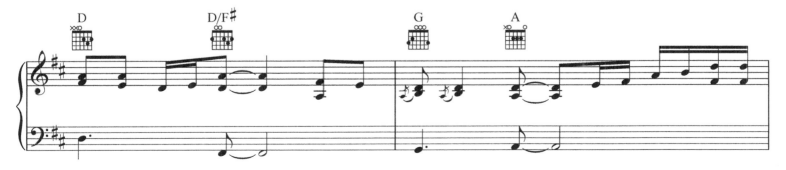

(La, la, la, la, la, la, la, la, la, la, la, la.)

D.S. al Coda

So, hon- ey, now, _

CODA

where we are. Ba - by, we found love right

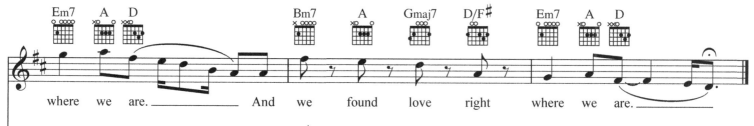

where we are. _____ And we found love right where we are. _____